The All Out Events Guide to Sport Event Production

Kristin Tara Horowitz
with Yishai Horowitz

2nd Edition

Table of Contents

Introduction 8
The Birth of an Event..10
The Mission Statement 12
    Who are you targeting? 12
    Validate Your Idea 15
    If Your Idea is Weak..16
    Telling Your Story 18
    Choose Your Mascot 19
Evolution of an event logo: 20
Where (and When) to Host Your Event...23
    Finding and Securing a Venue 24
    Permitting 28
        The Permitting Process 28
       28
        Finding out what permits you need 30
Doing It For Other People 33
    How Much Do I Charge?..33
    Do I Want To Take This Client On?..34
    Helping People Out 35
Considering Nonprofits 36
    For the rest of you . . . a rant:..36
    Selecting or Being a Non-Profit Beneficiary 38
        Charity Puts it on Itself 38
        Charity is a Beneficiary 40
        Contracting with Non-Profits 41
Finance and Budgeting..42

- Where Do I Get the Money? 42
- Budgeting 43
- Getting Started 46
  - Contracts 46
  - Taking money 47
  - Starting Your "Business" 47
  - Getting Insurance 48
- Creating Your Website 50
  - Building the Physical Site 50
  - What to Put on Your Site 52
    - Search Engine Optimization (SEO) 53
  - Registration 55
    - Exciting People 55
    - Minimizing Steps to Registration 56
    - Make Registration Policies Fair and Clear 57
  - Registration Logistics 59
    - What Can You Charge For? 59
  - Pricing 60
    - Incentive Pricing 61
    - Groups 61
    - Discount Codes 62
    - A Note on Bulk Discount Offers 62
  - Process Registrations 63
    - Things you should include in your registration process: 64
    - Waiver Production 65
  - What to Put On Your Site 67
    - Landing Page 67
    - Registration Page 68

- Results/Photos Page 68
- Course Page 68
- Charity 68
- Media Kit 69
- Sponsors 69
- Volunteers 69
- Contact 70
- A Few Final Words on the Website 71

Marketing 72
- Your Message 73
- Your Strategy 73
  - Types of Marketing 74
    - Owned: 74
    - Paid: 74
    - Earned: 74
  - Best Practices for Marketing Events 76

Pursuing Sponsorship 78
- What is a sponsor? 78
- Approaching Brand Partners 79
  - Large brands maintaining image 79
  - New market branding 79
  - Giving Back 80
- Creating a pitch 80
  - The Partnership Packet 81
  - Graphics 82
  - Message 82
  - Valuation of partnership 83
  - Partnership levels 84

    Prestige level partnership 84

    Mid-Level Partnership 85

    Budget Partnership 85

  The Process 87

Providing Customer Service 88

Developing the Actual Event 89

  Operations Manual Contents 89

  Setting Parameters..90

  Organizational chart..91

  Rules for the event 91

  Schedule 92

  Event Course 92

    Course Map 92

    Course Marking 93

    Aid Station Details 93

    Venue 94

    Setup Guide..96

    Volunteer Management...96

    Registration procedures and needs 97

    Timing procedures and needs 97

    Medical team operations 97

    Communications protocols 98

Sustainable Events 99

Contracting Third Parties 101

  General Contracting Advice 101

  Timer...102

  Medic 103

  Law Enforcement 103

- Vendors 104
- Staffing Your Event 105
  - Legalities 105
    - Payroll 105
    - Contract 105
    - Volunteer 106
  - Hired Staff Positions 107
    - Race director 107
    - Race Producer 107
    - Registration Director 107
    - Operations Manager 108
- Emcee 108
  - Venue Manager 108
  - Volunteer Coordinator 109
  - Hiring Staff 109
- Volunteer Management 111
  - Recruitment 111
  - Coordination 112
  - Working with Volunteers on Race Day 114
  - Volunteer Insurance 115
- Event Operations Leading Up to Race Day 116
  - Course build out advice: 116
  - Supply ordering advice 117
- Event Operations on the Day of the Race 119
  - Social Media 119
  - Parking 120
  - Registration 120
  - The Start Line 121

  Course Management 122
  The Finish 123
  Awards 123
  Emergencies 123
 Clean up 125
 The Aftermath 126
  That night 126
  The next couple days 126
  Three days after 126
   Surveying 127
  A week later 129
  A month later 129
 Failing Gracefully 130
 Afterward 132

Introduction

It's not hard to understand why you get into event planning. Races are put on by people who love races. Whether you want to share your unique vision with others or you love to make someone's day, event production is like putting on a fitness dinner party. All your friends are invited, along with all their awesome friends. The process is creative, exhilarating. It can even make you or your favorite charity a little money.

The problem is, racers and volunteers are not necessarily born. Professional event production is a strange mix of entrepreneurship, marketing wizardry, financial management, technical know-how, networking, artistry, physical labor, customer service, and sheer will power. It takes someone interested in a bit of everything to make it go. Sometimes it takes more than one. The reason event businesses fail is not usually because of the events themselves, but because of a failure to understand the market or a lack of knowledge about the business end.

This book is the product of ten-plus years of success, failure, loss, and gain. It is the result of a life shared by two best friends who eventually gave in and got married after going through all of that together. People have come and people have gone in our lives, but the two of us, and a few of our friends, stuck with it. We stuck with it even when it looked like it was curtains for us. During the hard times, we were blessed to have other means of support that allowed us to invest in supplies, infrastructure, and plain old experience.

Venue after venue we were told that we more efficient, polite, and better to work with than bigger, more-visible companies. We knew we had something to contribute and still do. We're giving away a lot of hard-earned wisdom in these pages, but the reality is that the people that need us either don't have the budget to hire us for consultation or they're too big to think we've got anything to contribute. Well, this book is our contribution.

Whether you're an existing company looking to grow or just thinking about undertaking your first event, we hope we can save you the stress, heartbreak, and time by giving you now what it could take ten years to figure out.

Best of luck,

Kristin and Yishai Horowitz

The Birth of an Event

Events happen for two reasons. Either it's a way to generate money or awareness, or you would just like to see this event take place. Most people think events are a mix of both. From the beginning, the smartest thing you can do is decide what the event really is to you. That will help you.

If you're doing this event for money, your primary concern needs to be making money. That means you need to draw enough people from the community to make it worth your while. It means not draining your time, money, and enthusiasm. Organizations looking to make money need to have solid connections in the community the event targets and that the event isn't part of a saturated group because you'll never cut through the establishment, no matter how awesome you are. It's important to understand the market you're entering – the participants, the culture, and the language. It's your job to learn that culture. Attend similar events. Talk to people who go to these kind of events. Listen for their struggles and concerns – be prepared to solve them.

If you're doing this for the love, be careful. The same concerns apply, but for a different reason. Events don't make money easily. While that may not be a concern of yours, losing money will be. Sometimes an event doesn't exist not because someone with the knowhow and passion just hasn't done it, but because it just won't fly. Another pitfall of "doing it for love" is that many directors are just racers that love races. You'll need to turn out something more if you want to be a well-oiled, efficient machine. You need to think about a lot more than racer experience or how awesome a course is. Those don't make a sustainable event, even if we all wish they did. Events succeed because of your business acumen. Great events fail because of lack of promotion and wasteful execution.

Keep the why in mind. Know your purpose before you do anything. It will help you design the event, market it, and keep going long into the night when your bed is calling you. If you're the writing type, now is a great time to start a journal and explore what you're looking to get out of this. If you're not, assemble a bunch of friends and talk it out. Take notes! Make a big ol' note to yourself that you can look at in good and bad times. Remember why you started this!

The Mission Statement

All this "know thyself" work goes into your first real action: **making yourself a mission statement**. Let it drive everything you do from here on out. It is your reason for doing this day after day. It is why when people suggest other things, try to hijack your plans, or get mad at you for the little things, you can stay resolute. It is why you stay on the path you set out to take.

Do not spend hours and hours worrying about the wording. This isn't junior high English class. You won't be graded on word choice, grammar, or spelling, but you do need to know what you're doing and make choices around this.

How do you do this?

Who are you targeting?

Set out the primary reason for your actions. That is "make money", "do something awesome", or "raise awareness." Determine who it is you're trying to sell to. Your event is going to be aimed at *somebody*. That somebody is going to shape the feel of the whole thing. If you're aiming for rich men in their 80s, your language and visuals, along with the course and prizes, are going to be different than if you were aiming towards a gaggle of teenage girls. You may say, "*Everyone* is my demographic." Wrong. Think about Apple vs Android. Are they targeting *everyone* these days, or do they know their audience and cater to them?

If you've never had to do this, there are a number of demographics research tools on the Internet. You can also ask similar event principals about their experience. For instance, it's surprising the number of women events are attracting, yet some events only provide male-sized t-shirts (shirts that don't get worn, don't get exposure).

You need to get specific with who you are talking to and designing around. You're not just saying "men in their 40s with road bikes." You need at least one other qualifier:

[demographic 1] + [demographic 2] = nicely focused audience member

Your event can have more than one audience, but you need to know this before you start as it will inform everything from venue to date to details about the event.

Questions to ask yourself:

- What is the age range (and median) for events similar to what I want to do?
- Is there an age range I specifically want to target?
- Is there a target gender?
- Is this an easily accessible sport with low entry fees or not? How much money should my demographic make to be able to comfortably afford my fees?
- What interests does my demographic have (we know they like to mountain bike, but do they also have a Honda Civic)? Is there crossover that I can target (e.g. do they just love minipigs)? Where do I find them (doing laundry at the laundromat)?

Once you start to ask these questions, you can do research with tools like Facebook advertising and statistics websites. Getting ahold of sponsorship packets from similar events is also useful. These demographics not only help target your event, they attract sponsors.

It's also a good idea to create a mascot alongside your logo. More on this later.

Validate Your Idea

The next step is finding out whether your idea will fly. Do this at every milestone in the event planning process. A lot of people have brilliant but brilliant ideas to you may not be brilliant to others. It's time to put your ideas out into the world.

You are now an artist. You are putting your work out into the world and others are criticizing it. We get it. It's scary.

Remember, events aren't just about passion and creativity. They are about money. You're either fundraising or you're making this your job. Just wait until you get to race day. You'll be forking over your hard earned money, looking back at all the stress and work you've gone through, and you'll realize that the only people about to have a good time are the people who came to enjoy your hard work.

So what is validation? It's finding people in your demographic, and then pitching your idea and price to them:

"So, I have an idea: [Explain idea]. Is this something you would make a priority to do?"

Listen carefully to their response. Then ask:

"This is how much I think I would need to charge for my idea. Would you pay for it? And would you sign up today?"

If you hear excuses like "I need to check my schedule," your idea is weak. It may not be a good idea or it may need refining. People who aren't ready to fork over money immediately are also telling you something about the event or its pitch. Don't commit until people say, "Yes, I am so there. Take all my money. I'll start training right now."

True validation is getting three people to buy tickets to your event the minute you tell them the idea. No amount of Facebook likes or supportive friends equal the power of ticket compulsion.

If Your Idea is Weak

The best products identify a need. This need may or may not be understood by the customer. In business this is called a "pain point." A pain point makes someone squirm. A great example of this is the mud run boom. It answered a couple needs in the general population, namely: "Running is boring," "I don't feel connected to people," "I don't do anything noteworthy." Mud runs are "happenings." They take a traditional 5k or more run and make something happen. Something which relieves people's boredom and makes them feel accomplished. Running marathons used to have the same power, but like any idea they lost their steam overtime. Now we have mud run marathons and more!

Sit down with your idea. Look for ways to fill people's concerns. If you're interested in running, ask the people you think would run your race what bothers them about running and races in general. Ask them what the best things are. Ask them what they wish was a part of that experience. Then provide it. Remember to incorporate those provisions into your message. Don't leave registrations on the table. If you have a feature, ensure people know about it! We'll return to this soon.

If you find you don't have a pain point but your idea is still not motivating people, and you need and want to do this event, pay close attention to our marketing section. A compelling campaign can make all the difference.

Where Will This Be Held

If you're doing this for the event's sake, you know your sport. If you're trying to make money, you may not. Now it's time to pick the needs for your location and pick your sport. These two go hand in hand. Anyone can put on a 5k just about anywhere, but to put on really awesome events the location should dictate the course. You want your event participants to be wowed. Location, paired with sport, is what matters.

Bottom line:

- Is venue location key to the success of my event?
- Can I find enough of my target demographic in this venue location, or will the event itself compel them to travel long distances?
- Just how challenging should the venue's terrain be for my demographic?
- How big a location do I need? Do I need to account for parking, festival, vendor space, or other space-hogs?
- How will I build this space out? Will it fill up or feel vastly open (be careful with open events –if an event is huge and so doesn't feel full, that emptiness can diminish the experience for event goers)?

Telling Your Story

The next component of this process is the trickiest for some and easiest for others. Imagining the finished product. What does everyone involved experience at your event? How does it feel when you're there? What's the ideal testimonial they give to you after it's all said and done? What features and offerings do you have to share?

In the initial stages, it may be tempting to keep coming up with elements to your story. Fight this urge. We will talk about this in the marketing chapter but, for now, just know that the more you have to say, the less your audience will listen. Complex event stories are not ones people will sit and listen to, even if there's so much more. Boil it down to one or two ideas. Most people do not care about the subtle details that will become important to you. We've had clients become obsessed with photo-op backdrops while expressing no interest in executing the afterparty they were heavily promoting.

Now it's time to create your mission statement. Be prepared to make all your choices based on this. something like a paragraph that you could tell someone while riding an elevator, an elevator pitch. You're now armed to make this thing happen.

Practice explaining your concept to friends and family. If they "get it" you're golden. Better yet, writing your mission down succinctly will help you connect with other parties down the line, from sponsors to participants to web designers.

Choose Your Mascot

It's time for a logo. You may not feel a logo is that important. That it may cost too much do make professionally. Wrong. You need an image to help guide your story. Whether it's a honey badger or a bumblebee, a tribal sun or a little lamb, a five-color graphic ready for printing on shirts or a hand drawn sketch by your beloved, we all need a little totem to guide our thoughts. A logo isn't just a recognizable little drawing. A logo sets the consistent experience for everyone. A logo sets the tone for the whole brand.

Remember, color *means* something. Search "color psychology" and make sure you send the right message. Is your event bold? Is your event calming? Is it tied to a location that's already branded? Can you can pull the colors from that? Again, consider demographics: a certain crowd like neon green, another pastels.

You can do some research on similar events to see what they do, but use that knowledge to do something *different*. You don't want to be one of a million. Eventually your logo becomes your entire story, even if it has no bearing on what you do. Example? Starbucks. If you look at their past logos, they were intricate and advertised what the coffee shop was about. Now? There's a giant green mermaid logo slapped on the side of my grocery store and it means, "Come inside to get delicious and consistent coffee treats and pastries from a company started in Seattle that set off a coffee revolution and is now conveniently in your market." Starbucks wins at branding with a mermaid: the last thing you think of when you think "coffee."

An early event company we ran called "Nimble Creative" ended up with a goat balancing on a stick as their logo. It was preposterously cute, but was based on something. It was how goats in the Middle East got up into trees to get leaves. The company name came first. Then when the logo got designed, it worked. We didn't need the logo to have running and biking in it, which that company mainly did. It just needed to be something we could hang our hat (or goat) on.

Evolution of an event logo:

We put on some of the first mud run / obstacle course events! But, because of this, we didn't really know what kind of personality we wanted to give the event, so we went with what was popular at the time:

2011 – commando-style/boot camp. No real logo, just stock photo of a badass lady crawing, camo, aggressive text. This is pretty common for event start ups in terms of design and 1st attempt.

The following year, we reviewed what the actual feel of the event had turned out to be, and it was a lot more festive than badass. People loved literally wallowing in the mud and having a good time, so I designed a new logo: "Happy Pig."

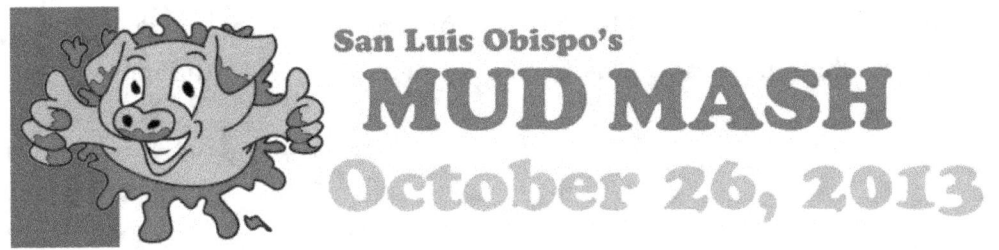

He's got his thumbs up, he's popping out of mud kinda like Porky Pig, the colors are brown, pink, blue and white. Evokes water, fun, but like . . . clean. I chose a more festive font.

And then while this event absolutely was "happy pig" we realized that to sustain it, we'd need to capture the evolving audience of hardcore OCR people who were looking to truly be challenged. Truth was, our event was every bit as challenging and well constructed as the "big" obstacle course races, but happy pig and the fun feel didn't appeal to them.

Enter, "Oink Oink, motherf*cker."

Similar color scheme, but black plays more strongly, there's a more core font choice, and the pig isn't giving you thumbs up anymore, he's about to take you. The pink and the black are like a mullet: serious in front, party in the back.

It looked awesome, but we actually decided that while it was profitable, it was a ton of work and we saw the trend of obstacle course racing dying out and got out while the getting was good. Our logos were neat, though!

Where (and When) to Host Your Event

So, you know "What." Now it's time for "If." You have likely started looking for locations that meet your needs. It's time to see if this is a go. Venue managers will need to be convinced that you're on your game and will bring value to their own work either by way of business to them, permitting fees, or exposure of the venue. Don't forget that event managers have to believe you can pay the bills, which means they need to buy into your concept. Think of it like an open house. There's a lot of lookyloos, but if the house is a find it pays to show you can move when it's time.

1. **The Ideal Date.** Knowing your demographic will help with this. Weather can be a factor, as will unique details like wildflowers and how busy your town is (ie, if you live in a college town and you attract college students, summer's probably not a brilliant idea). If you're attracting regular competitors, check race calendars and find out what people's training schedules are. If it's a school event, put it closer to September, when everyone is excited about school, rather than June, when everyone is over it. You may consider piggy backing on an already existing draw if the event compliments it. Remember to check the calendar for competing events at least two hours' drive away.
2. **The Ideal Location.** This should be at the forefront of your mind when it comes to your event. What will make people come to your location? Proximity to a city center? The natural beauty? Do you want to show people something no one knows about? Once you know the attractions of your location you can start looking for venues that fit your needs. Sometimes it's really just about finding a parking lot. In the end, it's not the beauty and quality of the course that keeps 'em coming, but the story.

3. **The Ideal Course.** Just as location should have been your true inspiration, now the details of the course come together. Who. Why. What. Questions like what will be physically appropriate for what you want? How much parking will you need for visitors (a good rule of thumb is one car to every two participants)?

Finding and Securing a Venue

Each venue works a little differently. Some will bend over backwards to have you there. Some will make fight you every step of the way. Some will be cheap, some expensive. Some will be a free-for-all and some will be rigid and rule-oriented. The key is speaking their language.

Once you have determined dates, general course needs, and the ideal location, it's time to start inquiring about specific locations. There are a number of options out there:

- Scout public locations on your own before you escalate. People appreciate it when you're already familiar with their property and what you want to do with it. The more detail and preparation you can show upon meeting the managers, the better.
- Go directly to the land management agencies in charge of a venue you are already aware of. Set an appointment to meet with them, talk about what you want to do, and tour the course. You may not be as prepared when you meet, but you may not have many options if the land is private or hard to access.
- Contact tourism boards in the area for recommendations. Generally, they will tell you of possible venues or put out the call for you. You'll receive solicitation from the venues interested.
- Get on the Internet. If you need something like a park or ski hill, you'll find it easily this way. Google Earth is your friend.

- Network. There are private venues out there that you can only find through friends.

Once you've got a couple of ideas in mind for your venue, it's time to meet with the principals involved. Some land managers have done this all before and will know ahead of time what you can and cannot do by their own policy or by local jurisdiction. It's awesome if they do, but don't always assume they will know. Depending on what you want to do on the land, and the experience of the land managers you meet with, you may have to do some follow-up research with the government or additional land managers to determine if the site will work for you.

Consider meeting with land managers a job interview. You will need to sell yourself as a professional (as you see yourself), your attire, demeanor, and preparation will matter. We're not saying to wear a suit, but "business casual" with the ability to do some hiking is appropriate. Don't be distracted, defensive, or unprepared.

As a rule of thumb, there are three ways to impress people: connection, history, and facts.

- Some people are highly influenced by the connections you have and the connection you forge with them. If you encounter someone like this, they will likely engage in small talk. Always look for ways to find common ground and people in your lives. They need to feel as though they can trust you. If you are not comfortable with this, there are tons of sales books that can advise how to get better at that instant connection. Remember, you are selling yourself with this person.
- Some people don't care about you, but they do care about your credentials. How long have you been in business for? What can you show in terms of your ability and work ethic? Even if this is your first event, you can shine with these people by being prepared with a general plan and even anecdotes about how you have handled things in the past. Some people simply believe that if you can outlast others,

you're worth paying attention to. Finding a way to dig into your past means extending your experience beyond that first event.
- Finally, some people really don't care about you. They care about facts and figures. How many people, how much money, what does the budget look like? What do other similar events produce and what's your plan to do the same or exceed it? This is where doing your research pays off. Remember your mission statement? That analysis carries here. It also helps to be aware of failures, to be able to say why those things don't work. Some land managers in this arena may have seen it done badly. Offer solutions.

Principals will generally want to know the following upon meeting you:

- What is your basic plan? (Mission statement)
- What is the date you're looking at?
- Who will you try to attract, and how many people is that? (Demographics)
- How would you describe your event? (Most people know what a 5k run is, but if your concept is a downhill bike or adventure race – they won't.)
- How do you want to use my land?
- Have you done this before?

Like any good job interview, you should have questions:

- Outline the area you'd like to use and ask if it's possible.
- Explain any specific needs like water, power, course or obstacle build outs, and parking.
- Learn if the venue has done anything similar.
- Inquire what the process for permitting is.
- Ask how the venue prices permits and what is/isn't included in that.
- Find out what will it take to get permission to hold the event, even if the permit hasn't been formally issued.

- Get to grips with how long it will take to build the event out and how much time to take it down.

These are key to your success and energy levels.

If they don't have experience in your event, some venues may need time to figure out some of the finer points. Depending on the scale of your event and the land agency involved, this process may take a while to dial in. Here is what you should come away with:

1. The venue fits your needs.
2. You know what you have to do to secure this venue and start advertising it.
3. The venue can fit your budget.
4. You know what you need to do to make this event work at this venue.

You will likely need to engage with one or more land managers for months. They request things like operation plans (more on this later), maps, and fees. Permit securing can be one of the most taxing parts of event planning because it's neither fun nor speedy. It is, however, part of the game. This is one of the reasons that keeping an event to as few land agencies as possible is key, especially for your first time. As you become familiar with each agency and its principals, you'll be able to successfully navigate the field and they will trust you a lot more. Events like adventure races, ultra runs, or triathlons may need more than one agency's permission.

Super tip: Learn the lingo! Everyone has their own specific language when talking about something. The more you speak that language, the more you signal to the party you're addressing that you know what you're talking about. Read up on these industries. Address issues like "ingress" and "egress" with confidence before they have a chance to bring it up and you'll be sure to impress them.

Permitting

In order to host an event, you will more than likely need to get formal permission from one or more land managers or land owners. The degree of difficulty in acquiring permits will depend on multiple factors. This can include, but is certainly not limited to:

- Event/race type
- Expected participant numbers
- Time of year
- Impacts on the land, recourses, other land users, local community and businesses
- History (has a similar event occurred on this property before)
- Parking
- Local laws or zoning of the property
- Ownership (private, city, county, state, federal)

The number one rule is to present a thought out plan that addresses the owners'/managers' concerns before they ask them. These include the above issues as well as a safety plan, an operation plan, and how the venue will benefit (AKA how they will get paid). Public lands are slightly different. Many park departments have a clause in their mission statements about providing recreational opportunities for the local and visiting community, so in a very real sense you are helping them fulfill their mission statement.

The Permitting Process

First things first. You need to figure out what your needs are for the venue and then find something that comes close to fulfilling those needs. You need to figure out who manages the area, or areas, that you would like to use. Then you need to apply or ask permission to use it.

Permits can range from formal city/county council meetings to a handshake with a local land owner. In all of these situations you need to provide a clear picture of what you are planning to do on the property, how you will safely manage it, how you will clean it up, and how it will benefit the land owner or the community it is serving. Provide the answers before they are asked. Be prepared to answer several questions, given recommendations, comments, and/or concerns regarding one aspect or another of your plan. Note these. Follow up each one.

Venue will likely have hosted dozens of events. They know what works and what doesn't for their location. Public employees may also be a concern. They may resent the extra work. Show them you have your end of things covered and that you want to work with them to reduce the stress of it all.

Finding out what permits you need

If you're putting on a small 5k run, more often than not you will be able to contain the entire event in one park or property. If you're producing a triathlon, adventure race, or larger endurance event you will most likely need to get multiple permits. For example, for our 24 hour adventure race we had to get the following permits:

- California State Parks
- San Luis Obispo County Parks
- Morro Bay City Parks
- California State University Cal Poly
- San Luis Obispo County Roads
- California Highway Patrol
- Morro Bay City Roads
- Morro Bay Harbor Patrol
- US Forest Service
- Cal Fire
- Morro Bay Police
- US Coast Guard
- Two private parties

** If you haven't dealt with permitting before, we suggest building gradually. Work with one to two agencies to start with and establish a relationship with the various land management groups. The most important aspect of permitting is being upfront with everything you plan to do. For example, don't get a permit for a 5k run at the local city park and then dig mud pits to turn it into a mud run. Ask first. Plan for how it works. If they trust you, you could get permission to do some crazy stuff.

Here is a checklist for land management areas and who to approach for permits:

Location	Permit Agency
Streets and Roads	City Roads or County Public Works
Routes or Highways	State Transpiration Departments Ex: CalTrans
City Parks	City Parks or City Public works departments
County Parks	County Parks
Beaches	State Parks, National Rec Areas, City or County Parks
Harbors or Bays	Harbor Patrol, Port Authority Agency, Coast Guard
State Parks	State Parks
US Forest Service (USFS)	USFS
Bureau of Land Management (BLM)	BLM
National Park Service (NPS)	Good Luck With That (just kidding, but NPS doesn't permit events usually)
National Recreation Areas (NRA)	Limited Events are permitted in National Recreation Areas - These can be managed USFS, NPS or BLM
Wilderness	No events in designated Wilderness Areas (can be

Areas	managed by USFS, NPS, BLM)

Detective work is a must for private property. Check out the local appraiser map through the County Assessor Office. Find someone who knows the owner of the desired property and see if they will give you an introduction. The latter gives you a personal intro which increases your odds.

The more permits you need to get for a specific event means your odds of success decrease. This goes back to RULE #1 in event planning: be flexible and always have several backup plans. In our experience, public agencies are easier to work with. They have set guidelines for how permits are issued, making them more predictable and easier to plan for. Private property is a different animal. You can simply ask a land owner if you can use their land for your awesome race and they could say, "Yeah, that sounds great," or "No, I hate people on my land," or they could just not get back to you at all. In some counties, events on private property need a Minor Use or Conditional Use permit. Don't go Rancher Bob and get yourself in trouble: check into the city or county use laws first.

Ski resorts, camps, and more recreation-oriented private properties tend to have a more organized way of evaluating and issuing permits than someone off the street will. Whether submitting for public or private permits, pay attention to the managers'/owners' concerns. Follow through with all the requirements set forth. A good reputation amongst land management principals goes a long way. Trust will give you access to venues, perhaps more delicate ones. No one wants to deal with someone that doesn't fulfill their end of the agreement. A bad reputation can sink a business.

Get well known enough and people will complain about you when it's not even your event that you're putting on. The public has the control, if they don't like you, all the networking in the world won't matter.

Here's a tip. Leave the venue cleaner than when you first arrived: that's good, sustainable management of your resources.

Doing It For Other People

This book was written with the idea that you were either undertaking an event completely by yourself (self-production) or for a non-profit. If you've got a couple events successfully under your belt already, or if someone has approached you to do an event because they believe in your talents, there's some things to consider.

How Much Do I Charge?

This is usually the first question I get. It's also the wrong first question.

You see, there is no set pricing structure for this industry. Get away from salary listings and put on your CEO hat. You're not doing an hourly job. You're contracting your life away.

Take your target salary for the year, divide by twelve, and let that be your target monthly salary. Figure out how many days a week of work that is and you can price smaller contract jobs by day or hour. This only works if you're not the one paying for expenses like insurance or business overhead. If you are, you'll need to make a spreadsheet to figure out net gains vs overhead costs. Come up with a gross number to start with.

Understand that you'll end up spending a lot of time in meetings, performing customer service with your third party (or event participants), and just dealing with what you did. Cushion your cost.

Do I Want To Take This Client On?

Many people wishing to contract your services operate under the assumption that their event will succeed because their idea is brilliant, that you are not key in that factor. You are. Your understanding of the event, the target participant, and the execution of the event, are all key to their idea working. If someone doesn't see you as anything other than a contract hire doing brainless work they don't have time to do, they will treat you that way.

We suggest that you look for a couple of key factors with potential clients:

- Are they willing to take the time to get to know you and share themselves with you? If a potential client has no interest in you as a person and doesn't feel that going to lunch is a part of the discovery, do not expect them to value you as a peer.
- Are they willing to show you their budgets and funding sources? This may seem invasive. But remember, depending on the depth of your partnership, things can get sketchy. We've had plenty of people sign contracts only to ignore payment schedules or payments altogether when their event didn't generate the income they expected.
- Never agree to a percent of the event income as your fee. Even if this event is your first, your time is valuable. If your partner doesn't market well or the idea is bad, you get nothing for your work.
- Look for prompt and responsive communications. You want someone who is eager to work with you.
- Look for someone you'd enjoy spending time with. Some clients aren't fun to be around, even if they pay well. Event planning can be very stressful in and of itself so don't let your client relationship get messy.
- They should be more than willing to work out a contract and sign it. Any hesitation? Walk. Contracts are like fences, they make good neighbors. You'll both know what is expected and what to do when it

doesn't work out. If they're not eager to get you contracted, they're not going to take you seriously and that is never worth it.

Helping People Out

A lot of people in the industry try to hold their cards close. We were once called by another event company in the area to rent some of our equipment. I asked if who they were. The caller was sheepish because he was putting on a competing event. Truth is secrecy and rivalry do nothing to help the industry or the world at large. Help people with their goals. Just make sure you keep working on getting better and better as you help other people and you'll have nothing to worry about.

We rarely say no to a cup of coffee for a "brain picking." They generally don't go anywhere. They might spawn blog posts (this book, in fact), event ideas for your self production, or creative thinking you might not get without that third party. Anything you can give away in the time it takes to get a cup of coffee isn't the kind of potential money you need to be worrying about anyway. We believe that only about 20% of these contacts will result in money, but when they do, it's enough to fill the calendar and grow the company.

Considering Nonprofits

You should always be looking for partners. This includes non-profits. If you are a representative of a non-profit, this section really doesn't pertain to you, but know this: you will enjoy cheaper permits, happier participants, and great exposure from your event.

For the rest of you . . . a rant:

If you are about to put on an event, be prepared for stress. Expect both untold hours of planning and investments for gorgeous buildouts and executions.

When you tell people you're working on an event, they will immediately ask, "Oh? What does it benefit?" It really takes the wind out of your sails as an event planner, especially if you're doing this as a possible living or simply to see it happen. Even when you do select a charity, someone will say this about you: "They're just money grubbers doing this *for profit*."

Let me ask you this. Why do people think a professional production, drawing thousands of people, closing down half of town, needs to be done by a non-profit? Yes, yes. There are important and inspirational non-profits out there like Livestrong or the Cancer Foundation, but did it ever occur to these people that someone somewhere makes money off those events?

Let's start with a non-profit putting on a race. If it's a small non-profit, it's likely a team of volunteer supporters. If you're expecting things to look awesome and run smoothly, good luck. Those people have other stuff to do. Larger non-profits may say they're putting it on, but this is the truth: they hired someone to put the event on. I know. Gasp. Maybe the team works internally, maybe it's contracted out, but if participants want their shirts there on time, with prizes, a fancy website, and efficient course marking and registration? Baby, you have to hire a professional.

Our business, All Out Events, is also a for-profit. In many of our earliest years doing events (even when we weren't called All Out), most of the time, our total take home for a full-time job didn't even come out to minimum wage. It takes years and years to make this work if you're the little guy. And yet, we're vilified for trying to become professional at this? What kind of a racket is that?

While we're at it, all of our events *do* benefit a non-profit. Some companies claim to benefit a non-profit, then demand a certain sum to take home to feed the dog. Our deal is that no matter what, the non-profit takes home a percent of our net profit. You know, that same profit we use to put the event on, and the next one. Sometimes writing that check hurts. It hurts a lot. When our day staff take home more than we do for months and months of work and fear of failure, we sleep at night knowing that when we claim to benefit a non-profit, we really benefit it (and that we pay our employees well and on time).

Why You Should Partner With a Non-Profit

Here are some really good reasons to partner with a non-profit:

- To avoid a rant.
- Your permits and fees will likely be cheaper or free.
- Participants may register solely to benefit the non-profit.
- If the non-profit is a 501c3 and you funnel your registration funds through them, it's a tax write-off. You're likely to get a few registrants for that reason and will have a better time attracting sponsors.
- It means you're helping someone.
- They can help you sell registrations.
- Alcohol/Beverage Control (ABC) permits. In many states you can only attain a day license alcohol permit if you are associated with a non-profit.

Selecting or Being a Non-Profit Beneficiary

We get approached by a lot of non-profits looking to be the beneficiary of an event or wanting to put on the event themselves. In the same vein I love to take what I do and help others do it.

Be warned that selecting a charity to benefit from an event is a big deal. If you're hoping to get help from that charity, you need to vet them. A lot of times a charity behaves like one – less giving and more taking. When you throw your team behind one you should be sure it sends the right message. You should want to work with them.

Charity Puts it on Itself

Charities who put on events themselves are either going to have an amazing return, or very little, if at all. Here's why:

If you're a large charity like Livestrong or the Susan G Komen Breast Cancer Foundation, you likely have the budget to hire the very best in marketing and event coordinators. There will be no holes. The event will run like a well-oiled machine. You will have a solid base to sell your event to thanks to a huge following on Facebook, a big email bank, relationships with companies who can provide exposure, or huge word of mouth. I can't think of a single self-produced event by one of these charities that hasn't succeeded.

If you're a small charity, you're going to have it rough. You'll either hire someone to put it on for you (and if it doesn't cost 50% of the production cost of the entire thing you're probably getting someone who doesn't understand the full scope they've been hired for), or you'll devote your resources within the organization to this event.

Danger, Will Robinson!

Unless you're doing a very simple event like a 5k, this will cost your organization a lot. There is a reason why sporting events are not usually associated with actual fundraisers. I try to communicate this to the small organizations that want to do what we do.

The fact of the matter is this As long as you are not working with a huge organization or you are not a huge organization, the event will be a struggle to make worth your time. Are you prepared to sacrifice your actual organization's resources on the off chance you make some money?

If you are a 501c3 (a nonprofit entity eligible to offer donations and sales as tax write offs), *one bonus to doing it yourself* is that your entries and sponsorships are tax deductible. People who do a lot of philanthropy will choose your event over others for this reason.

When a charity puts on an event itself, it needs to be sure that (a) the event aligns with the audience *or* (b) the charity's event is popular and doesn't try to compete for attention. Is the event's purpose to expose the public to the charity or is it for making money? A small, local charity is not going to have the kind of population draw it needs for a bike ride unless it has a long reach. Don't let your message cloud the message of the event. People like doing events "for a cause" but if 70-80% of your participants are out of the area, don't slam them with your quest to help a small, local population. It's likely not going to resonate and you'll have too many stories to effectively market it.

Charity is a Beneficiary

While it's great to benefit a charity - any charity – the cold, hard fact remains that being the organization putting on the event means you're assuming a lot of risk. There's two ways to give profits to charity:

1. Come up with a dollar amount for you to charge for putting on the event (say, $35,000). Anything over that gets donated to charity. This is the most popular approach, but for a slightly shady reason. Most times, an event doesn't make $35,000. The charity gets nothing, but you pay yourself. I say this is shady because if you're promising to benefit a charity, you have to do it. Unfortunately, what I think doesn't ensure the bills get paid.

2. Come up with a percentage of *net* profits (ie, profit AFTER expenses are paid out) to donate. Our sweet spot is 12% based on math projections about what looks good to us. Do NOT agree to gross percentages. If your event doesn't make money, hello bankruptcy! This way you ensure that even if you make nothing, you still have something to give. It may feel good to know that you contributed, but it hurts when you have mouths to feed.

My approach to this is based on what happens if it isn't successful. Building an event is like building a business. Most businesses fail. It can take a long time for an event to finally take off. In the initial stages it's key that you budget and make agreements with this in mind. How will you get out if it fails? Err on the side of caution.

Contracting with Non-Profits

While it's wonderful to benefit a nonprofit, there's a few things to consider:

- What your agreement for donation is, exactly (simple promotion, percent of net, flat amount?)
- What their role is (marketing, supplies, or simply cash)
- Protection of both parties' brand and reputation

If you are a small company with a small marketing and event budget, make sure your charity can help you. Volunteers, participants, sponsors, supplies, and co-marketing opportunities are all important.

One huge criticism we get each year at one of our events is that our charities aren't visible. If the charity wants to benefit, you have to weigh what they bring to the table. You have to encourage them to come out to broaden their base and overtly support your event. There's not much you can do to promote a charity if they don't wish to be present at the event itself.

Finance and Budgeting

Now the serious stuff. The money.

Where Do I Get the Money?

The little stuff has to come out of someone's pocket to start. Assuming you're self-producing, that will be you.

That isn't as big an outlay as you think. The event industry caters to after-the-fact billing for the most part, with some venues requiring a deposit. We keep a high-rewards credit card for just such purchases. Be sure you can pay your bills. Nothing hurts more than not paying bills, disappointing staff and vendors, and ruining your reputation. Don't Do It.

After your own treasury, it comes from registrations. You're designing your event poorly if you aren't making sure that the sales of registrations cover your costs. There was a point in time when corporate sponsorships were easy to come by. This trend appears to have gone with the wind. If your event is three months out, all the deposits and fees will easily come out of registration if you do your marketing right. If it's further out, don't expect much of the money to come until you get closer. Most permits and third-party contracts will not charge until after the event has happened.

When registration is open and you have some free time (ha ha), it's worth pursuing sponsors. We'll talk about that next chapter. Sponsors can be an important part of the fundraising of your event. Depending on your reach and ability to coordinate, sponsors may also be a major energy drain and a poor return on investment.

Depending on your location, another good place to go is the local visitor's bureau or tourism improvement committee. Their funds are a result of hoteliers self-tax meant to bring events to the area and get "heads in beds" during non-peak seasons. Come prepared with a pitch as you would a land agency principal, but also bring your budget and marketing plan. These meetings tend to be very fact-based. This can be a good way to augment your expenses if you're willing work a little harder to bring in tourism.

Budgeting

Budgets are difficult. No matter what you do, build in a 20% contingency fee at least for when things change. We've had last minute demands to double our liability insurance, expensive staff changes, flat tires on trucks and breakdowns. Random purchases you'd never imagine.

Here are the basic categories you should include in your budget:

- Startup
    - Incorporation Fee/Business Licensing
    - Supply acquisition
    - Brand development by professionals (logo, website)
    - Legal needs: contracts/waivers/trademark/patents
    - Services/phone line setup (if needed)
- Overhead
    - Bank Fees
    - Taxes from income (remember your income will not be taxed automatically)
    - Facility Rental (do you need an office or storage unit)
    - Owner draw (if you are trying to make some money)
    - Professionals (attorney on retainer, CPA, etc)
- Event
    - Sales

- Registration
- Sponsorship
- Expenses
  - Advertising and promotion (posters, website, post card, ads, even t-shirts and finisher prizes, because they are essentially perennial advertisement after the event)
  - Brand materials Business licenses/permits – this can be the biggest expense
  - Charitable contributions (based on whatever you agree to)
  - Insurance
    - Event liability
    - Participant liability
    - Alcohol insurance
    - Equipment
    - Employment (if needed)
  - Meals/entertainment (for the event – food, drink, etc)
  - Non-employee compensation (the band, day-of staff, timing, security – this is a big ticket item)
  - Participant Expenses (shirts, swag, finisher prizes, aid station consumables)
  - Postage and delivery (to mail posters, awards, etc)
  - Printing and reproduction (posters, day of entries and waivers)
  - Rental expense (equipment like trucks, generators, etc)
  - Supplies (course marking tape, uniforms, etc)
  - Travel expense (cost of gas/flight, lodging, and food)
  - Overhead (include this if you have only one event in place of the main subheading)

You may experience terrible sales and canceling the event is your best bet. Don't let your ego get in the way of your business sense. Too many people get wrapped up in the "awesomeness" of the event and stop trying to make it work. If you bust your butt to put on an amazing event and everyone loves it, but you lose your shirt, you'll resent the entire thing.

Check in with your schedule every time you decide to make a purchase. Learn to love your budget.

Getting Started

Once you've done all the planning, it's time to commit.

Contracts

If you are not contracting with a third party to do this (non-profit or otherwise), skip this section for now. If you are, pay close attention.

Do not do business with anyone who won't give you a contract. Ever. If that person refuses a contract, walk away. If someone is a professional, they understand your value and will not question you. If you do something because you trust someone, you will eventually get screwed.

Contracts let you outline your pay expectations, scope of work, and each party's obligations and responsibilities.

How much should you get paid? What's the industry average? Good question, to which there is no answer. You'll have to do some work here in terms of determining what the event's worth for you to put on – if you're doing it for free, bully for you! But that contract's still important. Knowing what everyone expects is important. If you're putting on a 5K with 300 people in it, you're not going to take home enough money to pay the bills, you're just not. Determine what makes it worth it to you and don't sell yourself short. People charge too little in the event industry and it's another reason why most fail.

If you're trying to make a living of this – work backward. Decide how much a year you need to survive by throwing out a number, weighing your cost of living with your cost of doing business, and then set a monthly income goal for you. Take jobs that help you do this. Eventually you'll start to know how long something takes, how much money and time you can save someone with your experience, and how much to charge.

We cannot stress the importance of hiring a good lawyer to at least look over something you've come up with. If you are getting hired to do this, ask for a sizable deposit up front. If clients try to nickel and dime you at this stage, they won't respect you later.

Taking money

You'll either need to contract with your non-profit for them to create an account to funnel money to or you'll need to start an account at your local bank. This requires starting a business account, which means starting a business. Unless you want checks to go directly to you, which is both a little shady to people and a big tax management hassle.

Starting Your "Business"

There are a bazillion fine books out there that tell you how to start a business. Here's the basics:

- You need to incorporate unless you want to be a sole proprietor; find out what's best for you
- The state and government want their takes
- You'll need a business license from your city or country
- If you don't choose to use your name as your business (Horowitz Events), you'll need to file a Doing Business As with the county recorder and place a notice in a newspaper
- If you do business across state lines, you may have to get special permits/licenses to do this as well

All this will cost you up to about $1000 if you do it yourself.

Getting Insurance

People always worry about this. They shouldn't.

First of all, liability insurance is relatively cheap. $500 an event, give or take, if it's a small one and doesn't involve bands or alcohol (these things are more expensive to insure). The real costs are the permits and the staff.

Second, it may be hard to find someone to insure you at first. Find a commercial insurance salesperson and become his or her best friend. Make sure they understand your vision. Insurance has interesting exclusions, like using water craft in a competitive mode. You can't always trust that the insurer understands that is part of what you do.

Next, you'll have to consider whether to insure your materials, like your vehicle.

Another interesting insurance choice is whether to provide health insurance for your participants. It's pretty cheap. "Cents on the dollar per person" cheap. A lot of large events force you to buy it and charge you a thousand times what it costs them as a revenue stream.

You will pay a deposit up front for the policy. It can be quite a lot. If you end up with more participants, they have the right to audit you and charge you more. The reverse doesn't happen. With less, participants won't refund you. Better to estimate lower and honestly and pay for more insurance after the fact.

Do not run an event without at least $1 million in liability insurance. The standard is growing to $3 million. If you can't afford the insurance, you cannot afford to put on the event. People can and will get injured, and they can and will sue your company for the cost of health care and other repercussions. Protect yourself and your assets, along with your reputation.

Many venues and vendors will not contract with an event producer who doesn't carry insurance.

As always, plan for failure.

Author Kristin planning for failure for an event involving a huge rappel. Back up and check those systems constantly! Gold Rush Adventure Challenge 2015

Creating Your Website

You have an idea, you have a date, you have a venue, you have a charity (or not), and you have insurance. It's time to tell the world!

Tiny events don't need a website. Most of them do. Websites provide marketing, customer service, registration, and the beginnings of your operations plan all in one. Do not skip this step.

Websites, like papers in school, also serve the dual purpose of helping you put together your entire system in a consumer-friendly way. You're forced to consider every aspect of the event as you lay it all out. If a website user comes to you with a question, assume you're the problem. Find a way to eliminate that question coming to you in the future. It should be smooth, simple, and clear.

Building the Physical Site

Not everyone can code, but as time has gone on, innovations like WordPress, SquareSpace and Wix.com have made it possible for someone to have a website they build and manage themselves, with a dedicated address (or URL) for under $20 a month. A quick tutorial, or simply playing around with it, and you're in. It may not be as flashy as one you paid someone to design for you, but if you're working on the ground floor, whatever you can do for free is worth it.

People will tell you to spend huge money on your site. Don't. Look at sites with races equivalent to yours. Most look homegrown. Even the ones for big events that draw tens of thousands of people. What brings people to your event is the message, not how flashy your site is.

Surf around for comparable sites of you're still not sure. Notice what you like and don't like. Get a feel for what could represent your site.

What to Put on Your Site

Back to the message. This is your primary task when someone lands. It should be clear on every single page of your site. *Keep it simple.* Succinct and poignant. People do not like reading. They enjoy skimming. Highlight key words that excite: *Challenging, energizing, natural, childhood, warzone.*

Interestingly, though people do not like reading, they feel secure when a site is well-built out (ie, not just one or two pages), but they only click on about three pages. So, in order of most visited, these are:

- Main page – where you tell your story in very few words and very good visuals
- Registration info – cost, categories, dates, policies, and link to register
- Venue – contains directions to and course map, along with expectations (such as parking fees or restrictions)
- Call to action – the most obvious thing on EVERY page should be a big ol' "register now" thing.

Everything else is really gravy, but people like to see:

- Sponsors – this is actually more for getting promotion. Potential sponsors like to see they're in good company
- Past event info (photos/results)
- Testimonials – for those kinds of people that need assurance they're registering for quality
- About (both you and the charity) – focus on need-to-know details with a just a little personality
- Training tips
- Related events – if they like this, is there anything else they might like? Be a good ambassador and make friends with other event directors. They will help you in turn

- Schedule
- A blog – this helps you build a following by having something to share on Facebook or in emails. It can make search engines direct people to what you've got cooking – even little things can be enough

Also handy to include:

- Volunteer sign ups
- Contact page – people don't like having to search to find a way to ask questions
- Media kit for media searching for info – if you make it easy, they're likely to use it

Remember that we all use Google now. People generally don't navigate websites by clicking through them, so the more info readily scrollable on a page, the better. At least for now. Just remember to put the most relevant and important info on the very first screen.

Search Engine Optimization (SEO)

This used to be a very scary thing to have to address. There were hacks and tweaks that could get your site to the very top of the search terms you wanted, but recently the best search engines use a combination of the text on your site, its established popularity, and the number of link-backs and referrals from other sites it gets.

So how do you manage your SEO?

1. Basically, you need to make sure you tell your story in clear language. If you're putting on a Western-themed 5k, you better spell it out, literally. Don't waste opportunities by putting key terms in graphics

that the search engines cannot read. Say it, say it again, and then say it differently.
2. Get friends, related sites, and blogs to link to your page. You can do this by being awesome and asking for it, or you can set up a referral system. Generating fresh content helps you stay on top as well.

We won't go into too much detail on this as it gets complicated, but Google has a free service called "Google Analytics" that can help draw a picture for you about how to continually maximize your SEO and target your audience by tracking what terms people search for when they land on you and where people come from when they come to your site. It's incredibly useful for a lot of other things, too.

Registration

Registration is the bread and butter of the site. You want people to land on your site and immediately sign up for the event. How do you do this?

- Excite people on the very first page with a succinct image or feel. This is a magical skill perfected over time. Don't expect gold the first time.
- Minimize the steps needed to register. Don't give them the chance to overthink it.
- Make your registration policies clear and fair.

Exciting People

Some of us have the talent inherently to capture other people's imagination and make them want to do what we want to do. Others don't. With practice, you can get there, or you can shortcut the process and hire a promotional company to nail this down for you.

Some tips if you want to try it yourself:

- Think *feeling*. Consider this quote from Maya Angelou: "I've learned that people will forget what you've said, people will forget what you did, but people will never forget how you made them feel." If you've spent sufficient time figuring out how to tell your story, you know how you want your participants to feel. Make them feel it.
    - Consider the difference between:
        - Bob Jones' Bike Event is a 10k Ride for Charity
        - Bob Jones' Bike Event: 10k for you, $10k for Charity

- The phrasing is key – one is dry and informational, the other taps into why you are doing it with as little wording as possible.
- Use second person – get into the mindset of the person you're courting and show them what they want to feel. I know, I know, your English teacher told you not to – this is an exception that works.
- Be careful that your message and the feeling at the event are consistent. You know that feeling when you see a movie preview you love, gladly shell out for tickets, and then find that the movie has nothing to do with the trailer? It sucks. You feel cheated. And you'll tell other people. Don't be that movie.

Minimizing Steps to Registration

Take a clue from the better retail sites out there – don't make your user hunt for a way to give you money. At most it should be a three-step process.

- Land on main site
- Click button to register
- Find registration information and policies

It's hard to construct something simple. People building sites tend to want to do it from their own perspective. They provide too much information. Some third party vendors ask you to create usernames and passwords before you get to see pricing. Some inundate you with text and put the registration button below the "fold" (ie, below the initially visible screen) so the registrant has to hunt for the information. Just get them there. Don't let them think twice. Don't give them get cold feet.

Make Registration Policies Fair and Clear

If you're new at this, you likely don't know what a registration policy entails. By the time you create them, you'll have lost sales from people who don't trust you enough to give them money and you'll have some frustrations from people who did give you money and then need something from you.

- Will you refund people who ask? Keep in mind you may have to pay to refund people in the same way you pay for registration services when they first sign up. You can save money by taking out the fees your service charges from the refund, or sending a check in lieu or a deposit back on their card. What conditions will the refund have? Injury, illness? How many days out should they ask? People will take advantage of your policies if you let them – showing up day of, deciding it's not for them, and demanding refunds.
- Many companies do not offer refunds. If you don't mind losing early sales to people who are put off by this or by angry people who get hurt, that's fine. Understand that if you don't offer registration transfers nor refunds, people will attempt to do unofficial ones. If someone is hurt on race day who didn't sign a waiver and you don't have their emergency contact information, that's on you.
- Will you transfer registrations? Will you charge for this? Does waiver signing become an issue when someone else takes over the registration?
- How will you handle teams? What if the team doesn't fill?
- Will you defer racers to a future event in lieu of a refund? What happens if you don't put that event on?

The simplest registration policy that costs you nothing (except good will) is to say "No" to everything. You've got to learn to balance work with good will. It all comes back to the kind of experience you are providing with your event. Remember, you can always be lenient under a strict policy, but the stricter and clearer the policy, the easier it is to fall back on when you don't want to deal with unreasonable people.

Registration Logistics

You will need to think through the logistics of what you're offering. If the event has multiple disciplines, distances, team sizes, etc, how will you collect that data and then execute it on the day?

What Can You Charge For?

Everything. You can do it one of two ways: build it all into one cost, or piecemeal it out. One, you get a higher price but nothing added, and the other, well, people feel nickel and dimed. What's the atmosphere of the event you're creating? That should help you decide.

Things you should consider in the cost of your registrations:

- Parking
- Admin fees for registration
- Stuff We All Get (SWAG) bag (t-shirt, etc)
- Bag check (if appropriate)
- Spectator fees
- Event fee
- Beer tickets
- Food
- Massages/etc

Pricing

Ahhh, pricing. The most stressful component. You need to make enough money to break even. You need to charge enough that people feel they're participating in something quality. Yet, you need to charge them as little as possible to make them want to shell it out. How do you balance this?

Research.

1. Go to your budget. You will know exactly what your breakeven price will have to be (remember to factor in the third party card processing fees and overhead of running the business of your event). It can be tempting to break down costs as a percentage of your ticket, but it will hurt when the commemorative t-shirt ends up being 40% of the cost of the ticket and tempt you to remove key event components, weakening your eventual product. Just figure out what it costs to charge and break even and don't over analyze it.
2. Look at comparable events. Consider their location and popularity in comparison to yours. Your event may not be worth as much because it is untested, smaller, or has less production value. It may be larger with more production value, but if no one knows about it, you're writing a check you can't cash.
3. Determine whether you're offering a premium event and that price should incorporate this. People will not value what they can get for cheap or free.
4. Determine if your target demographic will pay for it. Dirtbag climbers and college students have a hard time spending $30 on an all-day event. Established professionals will drop $500 on four hours if it's interesting and useful enough.

Incentive Pricing

Many events tier their costs as incentives. Industry best practice suggests four levels of pricing. A cheap, introductory price (usually your breakeven or a little less), "regular price" for the duration of registration, "late registration" as a penalty for people waiting too long to register, and "Day of" which is usually 15% or more higher than regular price.

Why? People like to wait until the last minute to register. You, however, need money now. You need it for deposits and you need it for planning. Get the money that you can, now. Early registration will only count for maybe 5% of your sales, but it's seed money. Expect slow sales until you get close to the "late registration" date. And then, well, it's on.

When can you expect to see sales pick up? Usually a month before the event, unless you're high demand and a marketing champion. It's scary to invest this much. If you've done your homework, rarely do you end up with a complete bust.

Groups

If your event can support groups or relays, you should definitely do it. This capitalizes on the number one thing that sells tickets: word of mouth. Your friend wants to do it and he or she wants to bring friends! Make sure your registration process allows for easy team building and ensure it collects the information you need from everyone. Work out team rules (maximum number of people, how will they be timed, etc). You can also discount team prices to increase participation.

Discount Codes

Many organizations promote their business through discount codes, some just floating them among fans and social media outlets, some targeting certain demographics (veterans/military/students). Most registration companies allow you to create a code that can be used with certain contingencies (number of times used, various price discount rules, etc) to take advantage of this.

Codes can be a great way to foster word of mouth among loyal fans. So be sure your price cut doesn't kill your bottom line. Numbers don't make an event successful, profit does. We like to have rewards for at-risk youth programs and military service members just because those things are close to our hearts and we want our business to reflect that. Do what feels right.

A Note on Bulk Discount Offers

A lot of new event organizers think that if they get the word out and the registration moving quickly on the cheap, they'll enjoy success. How do you do this? Groupon and Living Social and other bulk offer discount programs exist to do just this. While there are some success stories, there are a lot of failures. Organizations like this require you to price your tickets about 50% off, and what money you get, you must split with them – you're selling tickets at half price and you're only getting 25% of the revenue – not even enough to pay for that beautiful souvenir shirt!

Do not populate your event in this way. If you cannot get a buzz through other methods, do not waste your time.

Process Registrations

We highly recommend going with a third party company for your first few events, if not forever. There are few bugs to contend with. They understand what to ask of you to make registration and timing simple. It's usually a lot less stressful. As you get closer to the event, registrations will pick up. If something's going wrong – let the third party handle it. You have the actual event to worry about.

When looking for a company, look for a few things:

- Simple user process – it should embed neatly into your site and not intimidate reluctant participants.
- Dedicated professionals ensure your success – you sell, they make money: make sure you have an account professional.
- Social media integration – encourage your participants to brag and find their friends. Good registration sites have this dialed in to maximize sales.
- Instant and customizable reporting – saves you time on tweaking reports.
- Bigger companies can be a problem without the dedicated professional – but they have the potential to promote your product in ways like bulk emails and event listings. Take advantage of this. Their business will make your business successful. If they've done their research, they're good at it.

Things you should include in your registration process:

- Basic contact information (name, address, phone number)
- Emergency contact information
- Age on race day if you're required to submit or have prize categories by age
- How they heard about it (so you know where your participants are coming from)
- Team name (if applicable)
- Shirt size (male or female?)
- Option to donate to charity directly
- Waiver!

Waiver Production

Waivers are best produced by an attorney with experience. Do not just copy and paste an event waiver from someone else – the language may be iffy and not hold up in court.

A waiver is acknowledgment of the risk and absolution of the consequences of that risk on the part of the race producer, third party, venues, etc. If someone wants to sue, they can sue. The case may be thrown out – especially if it's based on negligence. Ensure you're doing everything you can according to industry standard for the event you're participating in. Someone could sue you for tripping or looking at you funny. Buy insurance to ensure if this happens, it's not your problem, but you are not off the hook. Be wary of the risks your participants are undertaking. Spectators and volunteers should have signed waivers too.

Super tip: Waiver and form design!

How you design your day of waivers will determine how long it takes to sign up! Good design's important! I've learned over the years from different organizations what really works. Here's an overview:

1. It should look as slick as everything else you have, have consistent branding, and be clear about what you're signing up for. Don't settle for generic. This is the first official thing people will encounter. That sets a tone.

2. Try to make it easy for your staff that is processing it. Include the most important stuff first, make it easy for them to check that it's filled out right, and find places to put things like categories, bib #s and amounts somewhere.

3. It's really great to put the waiver on the same page if possible so there's even less paperwork.

Run it by your registration and timing staff before you use it, and check in to see how they used it after. Keep tweaking. If you've got 500 people in line and it saves you 5 seconds a person in design optimization, that line moves 40 minutes faster!

What to Put On Your Site

Once you've got the registration processing going, it's time to populate your site and launch it!

Here are the pages you'll want to include:

- Landing page
- Registration Page
- Results/Photos Page (if you have none, add this for the second event)
- Course Page
- Charity
- Media Kit
- Sponsors
- Contact

Landing Page

The calling card of your event. If it's not consistent with what you want to be telling people, it needs to be fixed. Now. I don't care that you're busy.

It should have a clear menu bar for you to find other pages, a prominent registration link, your logo, and be well designed in terms of framing, rule of thirds, and usability. This is the first impression of your organization and your event.

This is what you direct people to for all your marketing. You can even have specific and targeted pages depending on who you are trying to attract so you can speak differently to each!

Registration Page

Give dates, details, and two links to your third-party registration – one at the very top and one after the details. Include a registration policy under the second link.

Results/Photos Page

Great for people to get an idea of what the event was like (and how big it was, how long it took to finish, etc), it's also fantastic for SEO because it's more words and links. If this is a first event, this page doesn't exist yet.

Course Page

People care about what the course entails. Provide maps, elevation, etc. Even if you have to be sneaky because of a secret course, give as much as you can. People feel secure if they have an idea of what is coming up. This can include parking procedures and how to get to the venue.

Charity

People rarely visit this page, but it makes them feel good to know it's there. You can have the charity provide content or you can do it. Make sure it ties in well and excites people who do visit. You should be excited about the charity, too, so just tap into that as you fill this page out.

Media Kit

Save yourself some time and assume you're going to need this. It should have a press release (there are lots of sites online that can help you figure this format out), downloadable graphics, testimonials, and other media coverage (the latter makes the media think you're even more important and again, provides great SEO).

Sponsors

If you have sponsors, they need acknowledgement. This is their page. They're more pleased with custom copy than just a logo. Always go the extra mile with sponsors and help sell them because you believe in them. This shows sponsors they're in good company and gives them a presence. Reality is that very few people click on this page (except competing event companies looking for possible sponsors), but it does increase their potential visibility.

Volunteers

There should be a clear page for volunteers to go and sign up. Include a value statement that clearly shows what they get for volunteering. How do you create a sign up page? One simple method is a description of needs and an email or phone number for contacting. We use Google Surveys to embed a questionnaire and track volunteers that way. Experiment with options – there are some great third party websites that help and many registration process companies offer solutions as well.

Contact

Crucial. Make your email, mailing, and phone contact information available here. You can keep it simple with just this information, or you can do a little personalization and show people who they'll be talking to so they feel comfortable contacting you. Don't forget this page – it's #2 after registration.

What if your address, email, and phone contact aren't "professionally" dedicated to your business? It's cool. We use cell phones and work out of our house – and we make it plain if people ask. Just answer your phone professionally at all times and you'll be fine. Services like Google Voice and Ring Central have ways to set up false lines. Email addresses can easily be gained by registering your URL and having all emails directed from the URL (@miscellaneouseventcompany.com) to your personal email address – if you use Google, it has a great opaque setup where people don't know they're interacting with Google at all.

Back to the site, the order listed is important. As a society that reads left to right, the best real estate is whatever is extreme left and right (or top to bottom). Put registration first in your list and contact last, and people will find them easily.

Super tip! About/Frequently Asked Questions - This is a change these days because people don't read. They Google. Get rid of your FAQ pages and as you find out what people are worried about, address it in your other content pages. Do it in an inspiring way. Every time someone calls or emails you, make a note to add it to an appropriate page. Don't worry the "about your organization" page. Nobody cares about you unless you make them. In which case, that's part of the story you've dreamed up and that should be integrated everywhere, not just here.

If you really need to have these, put them in the footer where people who are really looking can find them.

A Few Final Words on the Website

Be sure you understand your demographic well. Pick colors that speak to them, photos that represent them. Photographers tend to take photos of fit people, but if you want this event to be for everyone make sure your photos convey versatility. Unless those photos serve as inspiration for people with aspirations to greatness. Same with graphics. Pick accessible fonts and images that appeal. Research is key.

Remember to make your site mobile-friendly. Most people will tell their friends and they will look the site up on their phone. If they can't use it, bad things happen. They forget about it. Accessibility across all platforms is super important. A good web designer understands this.

Marketing

It is time to apply something you bought this book to understand: the real secret to successful events lies in savvy marketing. You can put on the greatest event in the world, but not cut through the clutter of advertising out there. You will lose everything you've invested. Trust me, we've been there.

One of the most costly, depressing events we've ever put on was also the most loyal one – when we killed it the year later, everyone asked where it had gone and how they could bring it back. To this day they're still asking. They even developed a fan page trying to convince us. Nothing convinces you like many tens of thousands of dollars of debt and disappointment.

The fact is events fail. They fail because of timing, because of mismanagement, because of not reaching the target market, because the target market didn't want it in the first place. Pet rocks succeeded in the 1970s, but would they have a hundred years ago? Or today? Why or why not? Not. Here's why. In the 1970s, people hadn't seen the level of "gag" gift the pet rock offered. It wasn't just a rock, it was a rock with a well-written gag instruction manual. You didn't get a rock, you got enjoyment. You got to be a part of something funny that everyone else was doing. You were a part of an inside joke with the world and you were part of a "thing," a "culture." The equivalent of an Internet meme.

And then we ended up with singing mounted fish, Snuggies, and the like. Aall of them made money, all of them are for sale, but they aren't nearly as iconic.

Hit the people at the right time with the right message and the right stuff and you win.

Your Message

Be consistent *until proven otherwise*. Do not send a different message with your advertising than your event or website. Ever. You do not want to be the movie every teenage boy went to because the preview looked awesome, and then they complained on opening weekend and it was a flop thereafter, when you'd really meant to attract middle-aged women. You won't have a budget for a redo at the starting gate. So you have to sell what you've got, with the same message.

How do you know when to stop and change your message? How are sales? What are people's reactions to what you're putting out there? What approaches get returns and which don't?

Your Strategy

We like to follow the Pareto principle: 80% of your results come from 20% of your efforts. You will at first have to try a lot of avenues to reach your audience, but it quickly whittles away. Find a niche. Work it. Watch it.

We suggest you check out the most excellent book *Guerilla Marketing* by Jay Conrad Levinson as a start. Read the book, take notes, and get to it.

Types of Marketing

Owned:

This is where your homework with branding and web design come in – this marketing is material you produce. Blog entries, giveaways, social media interactions. Cheap to produce (since you're doing it), great for building loyalty, but slow to grow attention.

Paid:

Paying someone else to get your name out there, on TV, radio, print media, web banners, etc. Though traditional it's becoming less effective in a savvy society. We don't believe you anymore just because you paid to tell us. Best used to create awareness and urgency – offer discount codes or value deals, give a stunning message, get out.

Earned:

This is, by far, the most valuable marketing. Viral videos, word of mouth, volunteer champions. People who believe or love what you're doing and voluntarily share it with the world. You do this by producing owned material and sharing it with what Malcolm Gladwell calls in *Tipping Point* (another book for your reading list) "connectors" – social people who have the trust of many and will get people to do what they say.

Ultimately, if you create reliable, engaging owned content to start, you can earn attention and pay for it.

Best Practices for Marketing Events

There is no right way to market your events, but we have found the following to be good starts:

- Table at similar, friendly events: set up an attractive booth with a raffle for an entry, a game for a t-shirt, and a slideshow of past event fun. Collect emails with the raffle and game and get them on your mailing list.
- Gather emails ruthlessly from people willing to give them to you. Send out a newsletter done by a professional mailing service like Constant Contact once a month that includes a little news about you and a little content that will engage the reader and make them want more newsletters. Always remember that you're not selling, you're providing something the recipient wants. Leverage yourself this way. You can collect emails and send emails before you have the event dialed – just engage people's imagination and don't make promises you can't deliver on. Make it something YOU would want in your inbox.
- Get your event listed on large relevant listing sites. You would be remiss if you skipped Active.com to start, but start searching for event listings – there are zillions.
- Set up a Facebook page and/or Instagram account and get busy. Look for content in the same vein as the newsletter (in fact, I mine my Facebook feed for content for the emails since we have more emails than Facebook fans and nobody sees all the cool stuff I post anyway). This has to be a bit of a hobby. You can set up Facebook or Twitter to deliver news and cool stuff to you if you know how.
    - Take over a hashtag for your event (#YourEvent) so you can see people interact with your event and respond. And find other hashtags that work for you.

- Make sure your social media content is available on your website, in your emails, marketing materials and other social channels.
- Make cards and posters. Old school works, I swear. People can be attracted by a poster. If there's cards to take, they can act on it later.
- Consider paid advertisements on Facebook. It drives the most sales of any other tactic we've tried, including Google ads. Facebook changes so much that we can't give you a best practice in advertising, but try it all. Take out different ads with different language and visuals and demographic targets and see who bites.

Above all, be sure that your website and your customer service demeanor match what you're putting out there in ads. The rest will come.

Pursuing Sponsorship

Once you have determined the value proposition for your participants through effective marketing tactics, you need to follow the same process in identifying it for potential sponsors. This is a huge topic. Much bigger than we can cover in this book – so this is a basic overview.

What is a sponsor?

It's better to reframe the word "sponsor" into "brand partner." The sponsor is not there to give you free goodies and money for being a part of the fun. They're there because:

1. **Maintaining an image:** if a brand is large enough, and established, it needs to maintain a big marketing budget that keeps it the leader of the market. This means maintaining the same demographic, the same image, and the same events. If you are producing a small event, do not expect Coke to get behind you unless you have a direct personal connection with the decision maker.
2. **Breaking into a new market:** there's nothing for a brand like a new audience. Whether it is just starting out and looking for an opportunity for basic exposure, or it's simply outreach for a new segment of the market, these brands are influenced by your pursuits.
3. **Giving back to the community:** if a brand is looking to be associated as philanthropic, the business may be open to partnership as good will.

You can either tailor your partnership approach or try a general approach that appeals to them all.

Approaching Brand Partners

First, how do you target each brand's needs? Get out of your head and into theirs. What do they want? What can they get out of the deal?

Large brands maintaining image

These brands are interested in big numbers. Low maintenance accounts for them but high for you. They want dedicated managers of the relationship, attention to detail, and proven return on investment. This is done through studies of branding, white papers (research papers using brand and event collaboration to illustrate effective approaches), and hard numbers. If it doesn't make sense on a cost level of partnership, there's no sale. Most start-up events are not there.

New market branding

These brands are interested in demographic details.

- Who attends these events?
- How much do they make?
- How old are they?
- What do they like doing?
- What cross-branding activities are they already participating in?

This is achieved by surveying research from established organizations. Do not guess. Many small events over promise and under deliver. Your first event will likely be your least lucrative event. You need the loyalty of these brands to continue to the next one.

Giving Back

These partners are looking for a number of things:

- Demonstrable impact on community perception (ie, a positive event that does something for the community it targets and takes place in).
- Non-profit associations (better if checks can be written directly to a 501c3 and the organization can take a tax write-off and proudly hail their deed).

Creating a pitch

Start with understanding what they want. Then tell them that you are the solution to their hopes and dreams. You will need to internalize a pitch in the same way you created a value statement. It's time to work.

Your first step is researching a couple of businesses you might want to approach. Understanding what events they already partner, what their mission statement is, and what their vision for connection with consumers is will help you take the next step: creating a partnership packet.

The Partnership Packet

At its core, the packet is the 6Ws you may have learned in elementary school: who, what, when, where, why, and how. Your goal is to tell it succinctly, enthusiastically, and persuasively. You're pitching to a real person who has other things to do and who you need to connect. In the same way you need to connect to the larger brand.

People are motivated in three different ways, sometimes a combination of them:

- Longevity – that's why you see things like, "We've been around for 50 years" or "Established in 1940." Longevity means experience, stability, and confidence.
- Numbers – provide demographic details, financial information, and statistics that prove your viability and makes you a solution to a problem.
- Character – whether you have a celebrity behind you or a strong voice that imparts a feeling of differentiation and trust, work it. Work it hard. People agree to deals based on chemistry. Determine what chemistry you want to project and own it.

Now, find ways to integrate this into your presentation.

Graphics

Choose graphics that present your event clearly. They do not have to be your own event. A photo is worth all the words in the world. Especially when proposals like this land on your target's desk every day. Stand out. Tell your story in image.

Message

People keep reading if the first thing you say to them is compelling. Remember that elevator pitch? It's time to bring it back. That's your "what." Then it's time to bring in your "who." Once you've hooked them and told them you can do it, tell them "why." Not why you are doing it, but why they should.

If you've done your job they will be begging for the "when" and "where." Give it to them in the graphic ahead of time, then again for the final sell.

Now the "how." This is a two parter: how you'll do it and how they can get involved.

Most partners want so see how serious you are. An upfront budget allows them to see what you're investing. Show them you've done the homework. Show them you can make it viable. Show them you're not relying on the partners to make it work – because if you don't get enough partners, it fails for the partners on board as well.

Next show them how they can get involved. This is a valuation exercise in what you're bringing to them.

Valuation of partnership

If you are a small event, or a fledgling one, and you have no numbers to draw on, remember this bit of wisdom: valuation of anything is based on past success. You may think you're offering a deal, but it's based on potential. If you have nothing but potential, you need to keep that in mind.

There is nothing wrong with offering partnership for free/in-kind, especially if it enhances your event. Find partners to help promote you. Find partners that were looking for ways to hand out products. Count yourself lucky.

If you have experience with valuation, or the event itself, then you can price your event. Shop around. Start with events that are the same size and type.

How much is it worth it for you to have them there (and deal with the hassle of paperwork and customer service)?

How much is it worth for them to be there? Remember that sending out staff costs in brand collateral, staff hourly wage, driving time, and general resources. Your price has got to figure into their backend costs and still come up worth it. Our best practice shows that for an event under 1000 people, the most you'll get is $100 for a booth from a cold-called brand that sees value in you. Even if it's an established event!

Partnership levels

It is a best practice in any industry to offer three basic choices. One is a high-value, luxury choice. One is your middle-road partner package sale, which will be your goal. One is bare-bones. This last one is so that you don't miss out on opportunities, but also helps you target your middle choice. Everyone wants a $10,000 prestige partner, but you can make money with more partners (and build out the venue) with much more accessible packages.

Prestige level partnership

These are title-event partners, like the Nike Women's Marathon or the Reebok Spartan Race. It's very unlikely you'll land more than one, so make it worth your while. Price it at what it would take to make an exclusive partnership work for you.

This typically includes:

- Branding on the event logo itself
- Repeat branding in all media and social outlets (specific numbers promised are good)
- Prominent and clear branding on event elements – printed specifically to include brand
- Custom branding experiences forcing the event participants to associate with the brand through experience and prestige loyalty
- Branding on all participant collateral
- 10 free entries
- 2 free booth spaces

Mid-Level Partnership

This should be priced to assist with costs. Don't forget that in-kind partnerships are useful, too. If you have to budget out thousands of dollars in refreshments, consider free refreshments a viable partnership. Value yourself at the brand's wholesale cost when it comes to in-kind.

Remember, this is where you should be targeting your efforts. Partnership management takes energy and you need to determine how many relationships you can and want to effectively manage and price it fairly based off that.

These typically include:

- Brand collateral on a specific part of the event (venue feature, obstacle, or other experience associated with the event)
- Repeat branding in all media and social outlets
- Branding on participant event collateral
- Custom branding experiences
- A free entry
- 1 free both space

Budget Partnership

For people willing to try you out and see if they get a return, be sure to pay attention to these partnerships. If treated well, they could come back at a greater commitment. Make these extremely affordable.

- Mention in social and print elements
- Brand on some participant event collateral (t-shirt, for example)
- Free booth space

It's best practice to present these clearly on a grid. Allow the decision maker to see the value in each (from their perspective, not yours) in your layout.

The partnership packet should be as minimal as possible with three pages in color being ideal.

The Process

Once you've gotten your packet together, it's time to go. You're about to embark on a simultaneous journey of courting partners, participants, and the media. All of them are related. If you don't connect with participants, you can't tell partners you'll deliver. If the media doesn't pick you up, your partner doesn't get coverage. That's why it's a simultaneous game. This is not a book on a winning partnership. Unfortunately there isn't a solid one out there, though there are a ton of wonderful sales books (check out *SPIN SELLING* by Neil Rackham to start).

Here are a couple of tips:

- Develop a short script and then call, knowing you are interrupting whoever you are, and believe that it's worth it. Ask how they're doing and get to the point. The point of *why they want to listen to you* NOT what you want them to hear. Don't ask for commitment, just ask to send your partnership packet and have them review it.
- Follow up with a polite, but short, personalized email with the partnership attached.
- Call a week later. They probably haven't looked at it. Remind them of a key reason they should. Ask if you can check in again. If they say no, *close the door.* You are not in the business of annoying people and you are learning.
- Success rate on partnership for a new event is very, very slim. Get your best salesperson on it and know that if you get a 10% "maybe" that's awesome.
- Partners move slow. You enter at the bottom floor and have to make it past all the static to get to the real gate keepers and decision makers. Some will not make it by print deadline – do what you can to accommodate them, but they'll get it.

- Some partners just won't pay you, even with a contract. That is life. Don't waste your time on them unless you get money up front. A partner that sends money immediately is worth your time. If you have to hunt them, don't waste your time.

Providing Customer Service

There's one rule for customer service. Be responsive.

If you have a Twitter or Facebook account, check it daily. Respond to requests quickly. Questions and feedback can help you improve. Don't think, however, that one person's feedback stands for everyone else's. Take everything with a grain of salt and remember that people contacting you are generally very enthusiastic or very disgruntled.

If they have questions you don't know how to answer, say so, take the time to figure it out, and follow up with that person immediately. Success in events means earning participant trust.

Sometimes an athelete's got questions and you're running a triathlon AND juggling twin infants. Author Kristin at the 2016 Morro Bay Triathlon.

Developing the Actual Event

With all the sales pieces in order, it's time to start developing the event. The smartest way to do this is to develop an Operations Manual as you go along. Create a guide for your staff before, during, and after event day.

Operations Manual Contents

Here's a typical table of contents for an operations manual:

- Overview: contains basic information that staff, participants, and partners would want to know, including what the actual event is for, what it offers, what dates are involved, and what elements are involved.
- Organizational chart: what person is in charge of what and whom
- Rules of the event for participants
- Schedule
- Operations timeline detailing when items get delivered/set up/taken down and who is the point person
- Event course: maps, details, course marking guidelines, aid station details (what needs to be there, instructions for volunteers), course map
- Venue: layout/site plan (graphic), protocols for parking/traffic control, food and garbage management, bathroom requirements, bag check, master of ceremonies protocols
- Setup Guide: includes start line, finish line and chute, recovery/vendor area, beer garden, fencing, registration, vendors, PA system, stage, power, showers, etc.
- Volunteer management: roles, instructions, supplies
- Registration procedures and needs
- Timing procedures and needs

- Medical team operations/procedures (this should be expanded in a safety plan or an Incident Action Plan (IAP) that is separate from the Ops Manual)
- Communications protocols: if you have radios, how do you use them – who contacts emergency personnel, etc.

Before you panic, much of this will get executed in time as you work with land managers, safety agencies, and your team. It can be as detailed or not as you want it to be. The more info the better though. However, the most important aspect of an operations plan is the delegation of tasks to your lieutenants. Each key volunteer or staff person needs to have a complete picture of what is expected of him or her and what they need to do to make your event run smoothly. It is your job as Captain to make sure your lieutenants have the information and are able to accomplish the given tasks.

Setting Parameters

You've a budget. You've an idea of what you want. It's time to create it. Those little extras? In the end, they add up. Number one rule of event planning? Stay within budget. You do not want to put on the event of a century at a loss to you. You'll be too exhausted and stressed to enjoy it. Keep in mind what your ultimate goal is. Do your best to produce that without breaking the bank. Do not cut corners on participant experience. We pay top dollar for quality shirts and knowledgeable staff because both of those experiences live forever – the finish line food does not.

Organizational chart

Give everyone a position and reinforce that position. One of the toughest things in working with a team is having people get confused about what their role is and ultimately breaking the whole system down. Manage appropriately for your team. This is a whole other ball of wax (*E-Myth Manager* by Michael Gerber, if you were asking), but be careful. You want happy, creative, motivated staff.

Rules for the event

Many of the rules will seem straightforward, but depending on what you're putting on, it can get complicated: if you're sanctioned by a sport organization – you need to know and follow those rules to the letter. For example, USAT requires you show a photo ID at check in (we are usually a little more laid back than that) and all non-members buy day memberships, with you retaining the paperwork . . . imagine how fun it was when one year we did online registration that didn't reflect the paperwork so we had to get all those signatures after the race to mail it in!

Other rules: for mud runs, what happens if someone can't do an obstacle? For runs: can people wear headphones, bring dogs, push strollers? What happens if someone jumps a wave they aren't registered for? How old do kids have to be to participate? Check similar event websites for their rules as you get acquainted.

Rule of thumb: once, there were no rules. Then someone did something uncool, so they made a rule. That's how we get them in the first place. Create rules that follow the spirit of your event! Why does your event allow headphones? What about costumes? Specific gear? If it's a cold water swim, what if someone really doesn't want to wear a wetsuit?

Schedule

Blow-by-blow of everything from setup to tear down. Be sure to give your timer an appropriate amount of time to calculate awards. If it takes a bit, schedule entertainment to make the time pass (costume contest, silly hijinks, balloon animals, drag queen – sky's the limit). You'll need to keep on this – we find that things change and sometimes it's easy to overlook what the website says and end up with volunteers an hour early waiting for you in the dark (oops) or disappointed racers when you had to close the course early. Make sure that one person manages the schedule and works with whomever else to coordinate how things happen.

Event Course

Course design will make a big difference to racer experience. Do not cut corners here. Find solid venues that capture the essence of what you want to communicate and make it shine! You're not reading this book because you want an easy, simple event that anyone can do – you want an event that goes all out!

Course Map

When you were scouting locations, you may not have made a map of them. Now's the time. The best way to do this is get a GPS device and map it out – get distance, mark interesting locations. People love graphics. Thanks to Google Earth and some photo editing software, you can quickly create a custom map for your event if you have some basic computer skills. People want to know as much about a course as you can share. The more structured an event (a marathon or a triathlon or a bike race), the more detail you'll need: distance, elevation, type of terrain, etc.

Remember what kind of feel you're going for with an event: are you appealing to beginners, elite athletes, or something in between? Will that hill be too much? That creek crossing too little? Get out of your own expectations and make sure you go back to whomever it is you are targeting.

Course Marking

Set a protocol for course marking. Are you painting the street with spray chalk? What color? With what? How big an area? Will you lay down flour arrows on that trail or will you stake arrow signs? How about using caution tape in places? How often? Have a plan and a lot of supplies. Then have the person that knows the course best go out with someone who doesn't know at all. Let them collaborate on communicating to racers where to go.

Consider this: when you are racing, you become a little stupid. The adrenaline's pumping, you're chasing the person ahead of you while keeping the other person at bay – you will miss signs if you're not paying attention, and you might not be. We have had some incredible off-course stories: kids local to the area going south instead of north on a highway who knew the course intimately, passing a police officer trying to flag the other direction; a guy jumping a taped off trail and ignoring a volunteer yelling at him to get back on trail; this stuff happens. Mark it like a four-year-old has to follow it. Leave candy if you have to.

Aid Station Details

Aid stations are key, even for 5ks that are flat in cool weather. The issue is this: people enter events because of the support they offer – both physical (in the form of water and refreshments) and emotional (seeing a volunteer on course and knowing they're not alone in case of emergency). We forerun each of our courses personally and determine spots where aid stations are best appreciated: the tops of hills, after a particularly strenuous obstacle, etc. Remember that many people are not likely as conditioned as you are (being an athlete and event fan) and may require more aid.

What you have at the aid station can make a difference. For structured events like charity rides or triathlons, athletes expect you to pull out all the stops with *petit fours* and *espresso* machines. Okay, not really, but not off by much. A 5k trail run can be a little more rugged, and that goes double for a 50k. Be prepared to supply liquid other than water, especially on endurance event days. Look for partnerships with high quality water mixes (such as FLUID or the equivalent) for both hydration and recovery and place them appropriately.

Be sure one of those aid stations is at the finish line, with bananas and oranges and water at the very least.

Venue

A graphic overview of the venue should allow for maximal efficiency of people flow. A lot of businesses don't understand this. Here's how it should feel: participants and spectators arrive, funneled into a reception area. Once processed they are released into the action, a sweeping vista of booths, the start and finish lines, a stage, whatever. Really in the thick of it. The start line should be obvious and the finish should be spectator friendly. Things should be arranged so that it doesn't seem like too much of a trek to visit booths or the bathroom. While beer gardens trap participants for legal reasons, make accessibility to bathrooms and vendors easy and encouraging.

Some more tips:

- Keep the food and vendors away from the bathrooms but close to one another (respect similar vendors and do not place them next to each other)
- If you have less-than-premium areas, you should do something to help with people flow to get people to those areas
- Put the vendors close to the finish line but in an area where they aren't blasted by the PA or band or BBQ smoke
- Keep the beer garden close to the vendors so they can get love after the race is over
- Make registration be the first thing arrivals see and the start line the second thing
- Have a plan for parking – don't allow people to park willy nilly in a field: it will end up a disaster
- Have garbage/recycling easily accessible by your participants – near beer and food for sure (buy cardboard boxes at garbage companies, construction supply, or party supply stores that can be reused if you line them with plastic bags – but the best thing to do is rent roll-a-way bins from the garbage company)
- Have at least one bathroom per 100 participants. The lines will be long before the race since when racers get nervous they need to pee! Watch out for wind with bad smells!
- Hide the generator somewhere where it won't be heard as well

To serve alcohol you will need an area marked off from the rest, enforced by security (and many times this must be a third-party company). The liquor license must be acquired by you.

Setup Guide

Take the time to do a build/setup guide with as much detail as possible for your team. Volunteers are generally low-skill in this department. They will need explicit instructions. You cannot be in all places at once, so delegating is important. Make it easy. Explain where *everything goes* and why. They may have to make decisions in your stead.

How do you determine what materials you need? Start by evaluating the course and venue. Will there be obstacles needing to be built? Signs made? Power needed? Volunteer shirts? Safety vests and flags? Generally your answer is yes. Create a spreadsheet with everything you can think of as you mentally walk through the event's experience. If you can't do this easily, attend an event and make a list of everything you see. Ask questions about what things are called. Knowing the industry terms means increasing the likelihood of what you order or rent being exactly what you intended. As you get in touch with different agencies to find pricing, make sure you save their info.

Volunteer Management

Outline the roles and responsibilities here. Identify needs, instructions, and be sure to include what you'll do to thank them – shirts, snacks, and swag are sure to please. How do we get volunteers, contact them, and connect with them on the day of the race? If there's an emergency, what should the volunteer do? (Hint: call their volunteer manager, not 911.) More on this in later chapters.

Registration procedures and needs

Explain the registration protocol from participant arrival to race start. How does day of registration work? Do you take credit cards? How will bib numbers be assigned? What goes in a race packet? How many tents and tables are needed?

Timing procedures and needs

This will largely be dictated by the timer. If this is your first race, hire someone experienced. You'll know a good timer if they ask questions you can't answer and produce a detailed contract. Ask them to provide this information for the ops plan so that you can be efficient on race day.

Medical team operations

This should be detailed at length in a formal IAP. A simple overview for staff to read and follow is fine for the ops plan. Be ready for injury. You must know who and when first aid is administered, what medical resources are available and when to escalate issues. Having someone with emergency medical experience is key to developing this operation. **Do not skimp here – I am very serious when I say that when you undertake event planning, someone is very likely going to die on your watch.** We've been to events where people have broken their backs bike riding or had heart attacks swimming laps in a pool. You are taking people's lives and livelihoods into your hands. You need to acknowledge that beyond paying for liability insurance. We make it a practice to remind our staff of this at every race. Let the medical team staffing the event make calls about the safety of obstacles or whether to call an event in a thunderstorm.

Communications protocols

Here is where you describe how communications are undertaken at events. Radios transmit to everyone on the frequency at once so it is easier to broadcast information to the team. If you have radios, list the active bands and protocols (for example, the FCC doesn't allow you to do certain things over public frequencies – like swear). Stay away from 10-codes and use plain speak as only law enforcement and other government agencies use it. You and your staff are likely to get confused. The other advantage is radios work in places where there is no cell phone coverage. Explain the etiquette involved. How do you efficiently use cell phones or texting? All of it goes here. Live Tweeting or Facebooking? Goes here, too.

Sustainable Events

We live in strange times. Most people are adopting sustainable living practices by trying to reduce, reuse, and recycle while events are getting bigger, badder, and more wasteful. No one seems to notice. This is a travesty.

To make your event green, practice these:

- Rent a generator and power it with biodiesel
- Use portable solar trailers and batteries
- Encourage public transportation, carpools, and bike transportation at your event
- Design reusable signage, event supplies, and obstacles
    - Cut weight in order to reduce transportation costs and save energy during buildouts
- Donate or reuse event materials
- Order local, sustainable, fair trade, or recycled products
- Offer recycling at your event
- Avoid paper-based operations
    - Avoid distribution of paper goods and opt for email promotions and online information gathering
- Make use of double-sided paper when available
- Get creative with storage and transportation – don't just have a trailer, build the trailer out for maximal efficiency so you need less trips back and forth and a smaller space.
- Use earth-friendly and biodegradable consumable products (like race cups and packaging)
    - Avoid plastic products in favor of glass or metal unless repurposed
- Choose environmentally friendly vendors (did you know you can purchase domain space from alternative-powered servers like Green Geeks?)

- Conserve natural resources by minimizing your impact and staying on trails, using natural obstacles, and recycling water if used for mud runs or obstacle courses.

Being committed to these practices will end up saving you time and money. If you are reusing and reducing, you'll find your bottom line increasing. The more efficient you are, the better time you'll have overall.

Contracting Third Parties

You've got the entire event concept dialed at this point, but you're going to need help. This help comes in the form of obstacle builders, traffic management contractors, law enforcement, food and drink vendors, medics, timers, and more. You've heard that phrase "it takes a village to raise a child?" Well, this event is your baby and you've got to build the village.

General Contracting Advice

Hiring for an event can be harrying, especially if you don't have a relationship established. Who knows if they'll even show up that day? We've had bus rental companies not show up at all for an event where busses were crucial to the experience and food vendors not bother to look up the event's location and call us, in an area where there was no cell phone reception, for directions. We've had bands not show up and food vendors not show up – prompting emergency drives to the closest town two hours away to form an impromptu burrito build for 300 people! That's why it's important to find good people, treat them well, and be loyal.

Some advice:

- Contracts – if someone asks for, or gives you a contract, and it looks pretty detailed, you're in business. The bro-deal people are not dotting their I's and crossing their T's. You will pay for that in the end, even if you're not paying as much initially. Contracts don't really do that much to ensure smooth operations so don't kid yourself. They're there to clearly articulate what is expected and what happens if expectations aren't met, that's it.
- Bid out stuff – we've found rental companies charge less for some things than others and used two different companies even though

they had the same stuff – and saved half what we'd have paid if we used one.
- Once you've contracted them, you need to get ahold of them a month and a week before to confirm they're on board and what you need is available. We've had rental companies rent stuff out from under us and had to scramble to get what we needed.
- Be explicit about your needs and instructions. We once hired a pump truck to clean up a mud pit for an event and the day they showed up, they called the city land manager and said it wasn't hygienic for that purpose. It turned out it was, but the driver didn't know that.
- Be flexible – when things fail, and they will, you've got to come up with solutions. Sometimes that solution is owning the failure and then bearing the angry mob. Never forget to turn to other local event directors for help or contacts. We've all been there. We'll help get 'er done.

Timer

Your timer is an essential part of your team. He or she will work intimately with both your registration team and your finish team. This person should be organized, understand customer service needs, understand his or her equipment, and be enjoyable to work with. He or she is one of the main faces of the event and can ruin participant experience with their professional or personal failures. If he or she is experienced, there will be lots of questions like wave types, technology needs, category breakdowns, etc for you. If you don't know the answers, look to him or her for leadership. Always try to get the timer to agree to post results ASAP on the day of the event at the venue and online that night if feasible – participants like instant results.

Medic

Your venue, state, and county will determine the kind of medical response you will need at your event. For example, a county requires all special event medical coverage be done through county fire department. Most other areas will allow more flexibility when selecting emergency medical services. The most important aspect is to be able to access an injured or ill participant quickly. That can change depending on the number of participants. For example, during a 24-hour adventure race the response time could very well be an hour or more. During a mud run, the ideal response time should be less than 10 minutes from when your medical team is contacted to when they reach the patient.

Law Enforcement

Depending on your venue and the local laws, you may be required to hire police, park rangers, sheriff or highway patrol officers for security traffic control or a myriad of other duties. This can be expensive. You rarely have much negotiation room here as the local law enforcement has established protocol of how many officers are required to safely control or manage an event. Keep this in mind when designing your course. Do some research to avoid the sticker shock. A few points to keep in mind: volunteers cannot participate in vehicle traffic control - the only ones who are able to do this are law enforcement or certified traffic flaggers. Volunteers can only direct participants. Depending on the county and state, you may be able to hire independent security companies to control beer gardens.

Vendors

You may contract people like caterers, photographers, bounce houses. The same thing goes for these people. Interview them for what kind of things they can do to help you reach your maximal revenue potential. They might be able to share advertising duties, split charges in exchange for free booth space, or provide you with free marketing material after the event (in the case of the photographers)?

Always do your best to do well by your vendors. Slighting them professionally will come back to you. Elevating them, helping them make connections, and becoming a positive network will come back to you. Do not engage with them if you can't follow through on your promises to pay or deliver by deadlines. If you do run into trouble, be honest and up front with them. Third party businesses that engage with event planners know the sting of a failed event and how it comes down on them. They will understand and work with you. Your success is their success.

Staffing Your Event

Having a team is crucial. You need good people who believe in what you're doing to execute it well. We spent years doing this as a one-two-person show for most of the year, but on event day (and on build days before and after), you're a team. Choosing people able to help you is part of your job.

Legalities

Payroll

The only legit way to have staff if you are a small, for-profit company. Is that person hired to do a specific job that you oversee? Do they do it at any other time throughout the year for others? Probably yes to the first and no to the second – a classic test of the need to cover your staff with workers' comp and insurance. Put them on payroll.

Contract

Many event companies get by with contract hires. Make sure the job description includes autonomous control of the particular position. If your volunteer manager has to get so and so done, you've contracted them to do it. Tim Ferris of *4-Hour Work Week* would probably E-Lance out the position in that case, and that's fine. That's contract work.

Volunteer

If you're a for-profit business, you really aren't supposed to do this, but every event company does it that we know of and it seems to pass the IRS just fine, but don't say we didn't warn you. Non-profit? No problem. Why is this even an issue? What if your volunteer is seriously hurt? Who covers their disability and health care? It's probably you.

Hired Staff Positions

We at All Out have a couple of basic positions that can be covered by one person or many. You may find you need more people or less, but the following is a good breakdown of roles within an event.

Race director

Without a race director, there'd be no race. This person is responsible for, permits, race course design, aid stations, schedule, and the medical plan.

Race Producer

This person covers the business end of things: insurance, contracts, marketing, media, customer service, and protocols.

Registration Director

From setting up registration online to designing day-of and mail-in forms. Even the registration process for day-of check-in. This person handles it all. They also should be involved with hiring the timer and coordinating the data exchange from registration to timing.

Operations Manager

This person oversees venue layout, course marking, and course building. They also oversee third parties such as traffic manager, police, etc. We usually have them be the contact for rentals and suppliers, and trust them with an expense card.

Emcee

Events can go on without a dedicated Emcee. We've produced and directed our events while announcing, but if you can find someone with a lot of personality, bravery, and charisma, they will completely make the event for you. The Emcee does a lot of things: they are the face of the event (many people think they are the event director/producer), they manage issues, they make the event transition from one part to another, they can start waves and give race briefings, they entertain, and they announce finishers and prizes. If you have a good one, they're worth every penny.

Venue Manager

This person coordinates vendors and partners, setting up the venue and hosting them upon arrival, making sure everything they need is available as specified. They need to be well versed in generator and power needs, along with anything else that may come up. They should be excellent ambassadors to your sponsors and vendors as this person is your main contact with them.

Volunteer Coordinator

This person recruits and trains volunteers. It's a big job. When the volunteers arrive, they are escorted to their location, given emergency information, and the volunteer coordinator checks in periodically to see that everything is okay and that the volunteers are happy and needless. Being organized, motivated, friendly, and a good leader are qualities a volunteer coordinator needs.

Hiring Staff

The event business is a wonderful place to be. Many people know it. Though we get resumes and requests each month whether we're hiring or not, it's hard to find people that are consistent, loyal, and professional.

We recommend vetting entry level positions by requesting they volunteer for an event or pay a small stipend for their work to see how they get on with the team. Most of our staff started out as volunteers who just wanted to help us put on something awesome. This made for a cohesive group of friends that traveled the country and stayed up all hours of the night.

We offer very clear guidelines in our pay scale advancement. We do evaluations after each event to help our employees become more skilled (and us nicer to work with), and after a few years of loyalty we offer benefits and profit shares. Many events live on the backs of volunteers, but after ten years in the business, we've seen so many people come and go. It's worth our while to encourage them to stay – some of them travelling great distances because they enjoy it. We make it worth their while.

One note on making it worth their while: because you are likely not going to be a stable employer, you need to make sure that the rate you're paying your important staff is enough that they are willing to take work off to help you (this includes travel and recovery days – if your event is on a weekend, they will be bushed at the beginning of a work week). Your staff cost should be the #1 or #2 expense for your entire event if you're doing it well and have enough people.

Volunteer Management

It has been said within the industry that your volunteer manager is one of the most important roles in putting on an event. He or she must possess a persuasive and likable personality, while being organized and empathic to the needs of the people giving themselves to the event. The volunteer manager typically recruits volunteers, determines need and placement, contacts them for instructions, meets and places them day of, and ensures their safety and comfort while volunteers are in service. They also release volunteers when they are no longer needed.

Recruitment

Who are you looking for? If you don't have specific needs and just want warm bodies, easy peasy. But, if you need good people motivated to work hard for you in exchange for the satisfaction of that work, a little harder.

Some people enjoy volunteering for things to pass the time or get their feet wet in an event without having to participate in it directly. This is awesome. It's how we got started – there's just something wonderful about escorting people on an adventure that's happening partly because of you.

We suggest you own this. Communicate it. All the incentives in the world won't motivate someone as well as making them feel a part of the day.

It is much easier to recruit volunteers to locally based events that your coordinator is a part of. Call friends, ask schools and non-profits. It is much harder to find volunteers if you're doing an event far away. What do you do?

- Create a compelling volunteer page on your website
- Post on community bulletin boards like Craigslist
- Specifically ask registrants to invite friends and family

- Contact service clubs and organizations for assistance
- Contact high schools and college
- Work with the local community service branch of law enforcement to give people community service hours (these people will not be super motivated to be there if they have to be)
- Provide great incentives:
    - Free parking, t-shirt, and spectator entry for volunteers.
    - Volunteer for an early shift (registration or course marshal) and run in an afternoon wave for free or a significant discount.
    - An organization can send four or more volunteers and receive a free promotional booth on site.
    - An organization can fill a volunteer site, branding it (hospitality, obstacle or aid station), with free promotional booth on site.
    - Racers enlisting four or more volunteers can get a race credit.
    - If you do a series, let volunteers work for race entry credit to the next event.

Coordination

Gather the following information about your volunteers:

- Name, email, phone number
- Emergency contact information (super important, you need to watch out for their safety, not just participants')
- Shirt size (volunteers should be provided cool shirts to way day of in bright colors for easy recognition)
- Self-selection of volunteer options and time shifts (make sure the time starts a half hour early from when you need them – volunteers can be late. Stress this)
- Special skills (nursing/MD/EMT or other)

You will work with your race director/operations director (if you have one) to determine volunteer needs. Keep in mind that as many as 50% of volunteers contacted may not show up. Try to pair people. Have priority spots determined.

Contact your volunteers a month and a week out to let them know you still need and appreciate them. The month out is to determine if they intend to continue participating. It provides information. You should send an informative email including:

- When and where to arrive (include a parking pass and map if applicable)
- Reminders to bring water, sunscreen, layers, or snacks (if applicable) – it's great to be able to provide most of this, but many event budgets don't allow for it and it's okay to say so, your volunteers will understand
- Details about what their role will be and rules if there are any
- How to find your volunteer coordinator to check in on race day
- Volunteer coordinator phone number for race day

You should print these letters out if the coordination is complicated (like at a triathlon or bike ride where volunteers will need to pick up supplies and drive to a spot off the main venue site). If this is the scenario you're looking at, you'll also want to have staff members who know the course intimately assigned to certain volunteers' care. For instance, in an Olympic Triathlon, we have different swim, run, and bike course managers – they will be the first point of contacts for volunteers as they can quickly respond to issues and needs.

Depending on the size of an event, consider holding a mandatory volunteer meeting where volunteers pick up supplies, are briefed, and have the opportunity to ask questions directly.

Working with Volunteers on Race Day

Volunteers will have varying skills. You will need to switch their positions as you meet them. Print out a spreadsheet that has your volunteer contact information filled in on a schedule. Leave room to make changes. Important spots should be filled by volunteers who are reliable and arrive on time.

How do you determine important spots? Where is it most dangerous or crucial to have a person? Dangerous or difficult obstacles, unprotected stop signs, confusing intersections, and lonely outposts. A volunteer coordinator should work with operations and race directors to understand the course inside and out and assess needs. Many traffic control third parties will have suggestions or requirements as well.

When your volunteers arrive, make sure to be at a prearranged space. We find the volunteer coordinator works closely with registration so we post him or her there. Volunteers come in, the coordinator notes that on the clipboard, ensures everyone has pertinent information, and gets the volunteer placed. Depending on the distance from venue to volunteer placement, the coordinator may use a bike to get around or else radio volunteers to see if they need anything. The coordinator's job is to ensure volunteers are happy.

If a volunteer incurs costs to help you, reimburse them on the spot. If not, make paying them back a priority. Most events cannot function without volunteers. Even if this particular batch does not return, you want your reputation about how you handle volunteers to be nothing less than stellar. People should be highly motivated to work with you. There is an event called the Run for Your Life Zombie Run – people actually pay to be actor-zombies on course because the experience is so wonderful. If you can make that work, you're a champion organization.

At the end of the event, the coordinator or operations director should sweep the course, releasing volunteers. If the event is long, there should be multiple shifts of volunteers if you can manage it. Even the most awesome event gets tiring.

Volunteer Insurance

If you are a larger event that's making decent money, definitely spring for volunteer insurance. It's pretty cheap – ask your insurance broker to look into it for you. Stuff happens and the peace of mind and care you have for your volunteers will be well worth it.

Event Operations Leading Up to Race Day

You'll need to come up with a plan of when things need to happen. It's good to create some kind of document that has milestones and the person in charge. When do you get posters designed and posted? Who initiates the radio ads? When do you buy your event shirts and supplies? At what point do you start to move your supplies to the venue and build out your course? In what order should you do these things? It's great to have a breakdown plan as well.

Keep in mind that things like contracts and permits may still not be finished. Keep on top of changing requirements and bills while you expand the scope of your attention.

Course build out advice:

- First things first: how long will it take you to build the course out for race day? Work backwards from race day and list out what you need done – then prioritize
    - Do a course walk through with principal builders and mark event element placement with wooden stakes or pin flags (if applicable).
    - Stage equipment – bring supplies on course and place equipment at marked locations
    - Course build out should begin immediately upon staging
    - Course marking should happen as soon as prudent – take into account if your venue is public, and people can mess with your marking, or private

- - Venue build out should be last – the details involved with the venue are not as important for racer experience as the course
  - Final course marking (make sure everything makes sense – this usually happens last thing the day before the race or first thing on race day while registration takes place)
- Make a schedule – evaluate your progress by how close you're following the schedule and try to make adaptations to get in line with the original plan
- If something is going slower than anticipated it may be a result of inexperience on the part of builders – determine if they need further instruction or help from you – remember that they'll speed up if they understand all the elements you're trying to put together for them.
- Remember that if you don't have time to build the venue out, it's okay. You have to play with priorities – it's event planning and things can go wrong or not work with the venue's schedule of operations. We've done registration for bike rides that wouldn't return for hours and had plenty of time to get the ride going and then build out the beer garden and vendor festival area. Conversely, you may overlap with another event and not be able to build out on schedule because they haven't vacated. Be prepared.
- Don't be surprised if you are building out well into the night before race day. This is pretty common practice for all event planners doing any complicated event. Pat yourself on the back for being initiated into the club.

Supply ordering advice

Ordering bulk supplies hurts. You'll likely need to pay before the event for big ticket items like t-shirts ($6 or so a shirt doesn't necessarily hurt until you've got 2000 participants) and finisher prizes like medals. It's important to find out what your lead time is for shirts, medals, prizes, and bibs because the later you can order these, the better. The majority of events will see big registration bumps in the few weeks leading up to the event and you'll only have a vague idea of numbers if you have to order out.

How do you determine quantities if you have no concrete idea about how many people are coming?

- Set a size limit for your event. Don't budge on it. If you've got 100 registrations for a 500 person event two months out, it's going to fill, so you know what to order.
- Shirts are tricky. You'll usually order too many or too few, and there's rarely a perfect hit. Too few and you'll have annoyed racers on the day of the event – if you promised a shirt to every racer, you'll double the shirt costs as you have to ship that to them. Too many and you'll have generated a lot of waste – though if they are designed well and printed on quality shirts, they can double as event promotion giveaways for next year. We work with a local printer that is kind enough to deliver shirts warm off the press to the event. They need two days' lead time so we close online registration on that day so we know exactly the quantity we need.
- What shirt sizes? First, take into account the demographics of your event – if 75% of your participants are women, please consider a women's specific shirt along with the standard men's shirt. Next, if you were smart, you asked for a size breakdown at registration so you can expand the trend to match what you expect to need. In general, you'll need a lot of women's small and medium shirts and a lot of men's medium and large. That's the best advice we can give. Sorry.
- When determining what exactly to order, remember that you'll have to either get rid of the extras or store them. Plan accordingly – do you have space to store?

Event Operations on the Day of the Race

You have likely spent a couple of days simply preparing. It's not unusual to work long into the night to finish out the touches, nor should it be out of the realm of possibility that you need to get up before dawn to ensure the event is ready to receive the participants. You may even want to ensure that the venue has lights available at registration and other tents if the sun doesn't rise before your team and volunteers are scheduled to arrive.

It's best to have an event-day briefing with your staff before it gets crazy. This is a great time to check in with the team to ensure everyone feels good about what is going to happen and knows what to do if things don't go well (unexpected things happen).

Event staff should be equipped with emergency procedure knowledge, course knowledge, and food and water supplied throughout the day so they can continue to be effective. Allow for a quick meeting and then allow the parties to disburse to wherever they're most needed.

Social Media

Get your social media admins mobile access and have them post images and updates as exciting things happen throughout the day – it's a great way to build spectator excitement online and encourage people to come out if they haven't already.

Parking

Parking is likely your first point of contact with your participants. Ensure that those who have prepaid for passes have ample time to print and bring them along. Prepare a list in case they forget. Many of our events require assisted parking staff to keep car lines in order Others require orderly bus loading to get to the main event. Ensuring trustworthy staff are here on the first contact is important. Early morning frustration can lead to a terrible experience even if everything else goes well.

Registration

Your registration coordinator should have worked with your timer (if you have one) to figure out a registration packet distribution system. If you have timing chips or bibs, they can be handed out separately or prepacked with other race packet information such as schedules, programs, SWAG, or beer tickets. We do not recommend prepacking shirts in the packets as they are bulky and make packet storage problematic, especially for large teams.

We've tried a number of systems with regard to packet pickup and the following are our best practices depending on the kind of event:

- Small events (under 1000) with solo participants such as runs, bike rides, or triathlons have packets arranged by last name.
- Small events with teams and solos have packets arranged by team name or last name.
- Large events have a kiosk posted with bib numbers available sorted by last name of participant – that way the participant can get in line with minimal confusion about what to look up.

Registration coordinator should have packets sorted in organizers, shirts (if not already in the packets) sorted behind them by size and sex for easy collection, and at least two manifests. One, with all information available (including emergency contact info) in case of problems, and a second with a check-in slip by last name, team name, and bib number to look people up who are not sure where they belong. There can be a number of these, depending on number of participants. Online registration software companies are increasingly offering check-in services using tablet computers, and we encourage you to look into that system as well.

For every 300 participants, we have three volunteers work registration. One to call out bib numbers off the list and receive the participant, one to pull the packet and timing chips (if needed), and one to pull shirts. Lines are inevitable. A dialed system can make them go a lot faster.

We maintain that same ratio if you take day-of registration – the more experienced volunteers (or the registration coordinator) should run this to ensure everything is in order. We used iPads with Register to process sales (but still use paper forms to process the info for speed purposes), though many registration process companies are starting to offer integrated day of registration purchasing.

For large events, you'll need someone periodically expediting the lines. If lines become too long people won't be able to figure out the lines. Some may get into a long line they aren't supposed to be in. We also use stove pipe delineators (big orange cones that are used for road construction) wrapped with rope or tape to make temporary and mobile lines.

The Start Line

The next likely activity a racer will do is find the start line and get ready to go. It's a great idea to have your portapotties nearby. Racers are generally nervous before the event and will need to relieve themselves a disproportionate amount of times compared to a normal day. Human nature!

It's a great idea to station the EmCee there (if you have one) or Race Director. Have him or her give a race briefing at least fifteen minutes before the event.

The race briefing should include:

- Sponsor information
- Race rules and hazards to look out for
- Motivation
- Gratitude to anyone appropriate

When it's time to start, make an announcement. Start your countdown and. . . They're off! Depending on your event, you may have a lot of waiting around to do (ahem, 12-hour backcountry adventure races), or you might need to start the process all over again for events with waves.

Course Management

Once racers are on course, your volunteers and operations coordinator jump to work. The two parties should work together to communicate course breakdowns, course marking failures, and injuries. The race director deals with the higher level "we need you to make a call" on this. With a capable team, this doesn't need to happen during the event very often. This means the race director falls to a "fixer" and "Honey-Do" position, getting extra cups for aid stations or securing supplies to fix problems on course.

The Finish

As racers come through the finish, be sure someone is there to greet them! It should feel like a party as much for the winner as for the final finisher. Do your best not to let your EmCee talk over people's finish experiences. Each person is having a deeply personal event and your job is to make it feel that way.

Finish line workers will hand out finisher prizes, cut timing chips off shoes, or what have you. They are also there to assist event participants with questions and recovery areas.

Awards

There's no way around it. Awards suck. People really like deep prize categories by age because that means more chances at bragging rights. That also makes for a very long awards ceremony. That's if your timer has lived up to his or her promise and gotten you the results quickly and correctly.

Do your best to be both quick and entertaining during awards. Make sure to highlight participants as they receive awards equally. If participants have gone home before receiving their awards, don't feel slighted – tease that empty podium!

Emergencies

We said it before and we'll say it again. Plan for emergency. As a race director or producer get formal medical training. Not so that you can attend to injuries but so you can make intelligent calls on your race victims. Look into Wilderness First Aid training as a first step. Within a weekend you will be versed in what to do in the case of injuries that look a lot like what you'll encounter – breaks, allergic reactions, sprains, etc.

Beyond that, hire emergency technicians you trust. Some people do it freelance and some do it with an organization (and some venues require a certain organization be hired for this reason of trust). Make it clear on race day that they have the power to close the race down for the best interest of racers. We've had them call events on account of lightning storms and pull obstacles they consider dangerous after multiple participants were injured. They are likely used to fighting with event directors who do not put safety as a number one priority. Make sure they understand that you are different. Back it up. Do not go forward with an event element that your medical staff doesn't trust.

When emergencies arise, have the people on course notify either the course director or volunteer coordinator. These people should be able to make a quick determination about what's best for the victim – even if that's just calling the on-site medical or race director for further evaluation. Do not advise anyone call 911. If they do on their own, great, but 911 can gum up the existing operations plan, and you SHOULD have emergency response available for your event onsite, so get a faster turnaround time anyway. Allow your medical staff to handle dispatching of medical services.

Clean up

Even long events sometimes required immediate cleanup at the end of the race. Not so bad for a 10k trail run, but pretty awful for a mud run or triathlon. Your best bet is to have a clean-up crew to ensure your staff doesn't burn out. These people can be temporary hired muscle, but you'll need at least a few coordinators to make sure nothing's forgotten and everything is loaded properly.

The reality is that you're likely going to end up doing it yourself. While your participants bask in the awesomeness you've provided, you might be slogging away taking down bike racks and collecting cones and microtrash in the venue (What's microtrash? Wrapper pieces and cigarette butts). It hurts. It really hurts. But you've got to do it. Why? Because your main job now is to show the public and the venue managers that you are responsible and worth continuing a relationship with.

One other great way to minimize the pain of pack up is to figure out a way to postpone cleanup for one day. Coming back well rested makes a big difference if you've been working hard all week only to be in a hurry to clean up. Venue selection comes a long way in solving this problem – if they can allow you time to recover, so much the better.

The Aftermath

The event is over. Everyone's gone home and you're either packing up all the stuff or you've just finished it. Now what?

That night

- Post your results on your website. Let people know they're up via social media if you use it.
- Sleep (this is fairly important from time to time).

The next couple days

- Sleep in.
- Go to breakfast.
- Lay around if you can. Otherwise, keep packing stuff up.
- Answer all the results questions you'll get and make updates accordingly.
- Sleep. (You think I'm kidding, don't you? I'm not. You'll want to lie around for days. It's okay.)

Three days after

- Collect all your lost and found stuff – take a photo of it.
- Enter all the emails you collected from the day of registration (if you did that) and enter them into a contact spreadsheet for sending emails.
- Get links from your photographers for the photos.
- Make a survey.
- Send an email containing all this.

Surveying

Surveying your participants is crucial to the process, even though many companies decide not to do this. Here's why: wonderful feedback will make you feel amazing and rejuvenated if you are worn out from your efforts. You will also get wonderful feedback about the racers' actual experience and therefore improve on your skills and the next event. Sometimes you'll also get horrible feedback from cranky people. It may help you design an event that makes cranky people not come. You think I'm joking, but I'm not. We had a triathlon that got a lot of cranky people and we changed the marketing on it – they complained it was too rugged – so it became the rugged triathlon. Let your participants help you shape your story and your event.

How do you do this? Ask them. Here's what we've determined are the best general question to ask (add more if you have ones you think are missing!):

- What were your perceptions before you entered and were you reluctant to register in any way? (You'll get an idea for how strong that story is we told you to create.)
- How did you feel once you finished? (This is great testimonial material and adds to your story. One time we had someone tell us they felt like they could eat the moon and kill all the terrorists. That still makes me happy. Surveys are awesome.)
- What motivates you to register for an event like this? (Ask and ye shall receive!)
- What is your level of satisfaction with the event (from very satisfied to very dissatisfied)?
- Please rank the importance of the following elements of the event:
    - Price
    - Location
    - Date/Season offered
    - Challenging course

        - Length of course
        - Number of participants
        - Other
    - Rate on a scale of 1 to 5 how you felt about the event experience
        - Registration
        - Course
        - Post-event festival
        - Value received
    - How likely are you to attend this event again?
    - How likely are you to recommend this event to a friend of colleague?
    - What was your best event experience? (Warm fuzzies!)
    - What was your worst event experience? (Honesty!)
    - How did you find out about us?
    - How did we compare to similar events?
    - How far would you travel for a similar event?

Always make room for comments. People who respond care about what they're trying to share with you, and you should too. These people help refine your work and they get nothing out of doing it for you (unless you want to promote the survey with a discount or something for more respondents). Don't feel bad about only getting a 10% response rate. You'll generally hear from the most supportive and most upset and a few in between. Don't think everything you see in response is law, but it's a good indication.

Once you have this built (Survey Monkey does this for free, but you can't ask that many questions. We use Constant Contact), you'll want to email your participants with photos, results, coupons, and a link to the survey, thanking them for being a part of something amazing.

A week later

- Keep lying there.
- Take your team out to dinner and have a "lessons learned" discussion with them about three things: what you did great, what needs improvement, what never should happen again. Write it down somewhere you won't lose it. You need to look at this a lot if you repeat the event next year. Give them paychecks.
- Write checks to all your vendors.

A month later

- You or your bookkeeper should now have all your expenses in and you can analyze how you did. Is it time to end your event career or launch it? Will you commit to another event next year? If so, ride the high of all those people that liked the event and open up registration! And repeat the whole process!
- Write charity checks (depending on how you worked that out) and 'thank yous' to sponsors and people who helped.

Congratulations, you are now an experienced race director!

Failing Gracefully

We had to add this section because failure in the event world is common. People often make the assumption that because a business exists or that it's getting media coverage, that it must be working. We here at All Out Events have had our share of business failures . . . and almost every week we're contacted by someone that misses an event we put on that no longer exists.

We were interviewed for our university alumni magazine and while it's a great honor to be in the alum newsletter alongside real change makers and astronauts, when it came out, it gave people the impression that we were pure success, rolling in dollar bills, when nothing could be further from the truth. It's been a long, slow growth with a lot of backward steps.

The fact of the matter is that events cost a lot to put on. You really need to understand how to reach your target audience. You need to nail the execution and keep people safe. Stuff happens. These things happen. Sometimes it's your fault. Sometimes it's not.

Done right, it's hard to turn a profit on events while keeping people safe. Many individuals just starting out don't understand it. Heck, ten years in the event and tourism industry and we've made some bad mistakes the whole way through – over extending our calendars, not calculating our budget right, relying on promises instead of what's in a contract . . . but happily we've had enough successes that it balances out and we're able to keep going and growing.

It's embarrassing to fail after making big promises. It's heartbreaking to lose huge money on an event you put your heart and soul into for a long time in planning. We get it. But don't jerk your participants around. If you can't pay your bills, tell them so. Make it a priority to return their money to them. If you think you can get it together next year, offer them a free entry next year with the credit but give them their money when it's clear the next event's a no-go.

If you have to cancel an event, don't lie about why. If you have to offer less to your participants, say so. Explain it.

If you can't pay your vendors, tell them immediately and come up with a plan.

We live in a world that encourages lying and bamboozling to save face and money. Don't be a part of that. Events are about people, first and foremost. The best thing on event day is helping people have the time of their lives on the sweat of your back. If you can't do that for them, you should remember why you're doing this in the first place. Put people first.

And if you're here just to capitalize on a commodity, go home. If you're not willing to cry over this, it's not for you. Yes, you should take care of yourself, yes, you should be making money, but you'll fail because you don't understand what you're doing. You'll leave a wake of unhappy vendors and participants that will follow you well past bankruptcy. People will remain loyal if you're honest and real with them. They'll give you another chance to do it right.

Failure helps us learn and grow, but only if you fail gracefully.

Afterward

It is our sincere hope that you found this book useful. You can find more information at our website, including free downloads and ways to contact us for more information or questions. We're always looking to help, get better, and do cool things. And we LOVE hearing how we've been able to help!

You can find us at: AllOutEvents.com

Happy event production!

Kristin and Yishai Horowitz and the whole All Out Events team